MORE TASTE

Annie Bell began her cookery career with a hands-on spell in the kitchen, first by setting up the small café at the back of the specialist bookshop Books for Cooks, and subsequently working as a chef. Children changed all that, and she is now a full-time author and journalist. She writes on food and cookery for the *Independent* (shortlisted for the Glenfiddich Awards in 1996), and was cookery writer on *Vogue* from 1992–95. She continues to specialise in vegetarian cookery, and is one of the principal exponents in the UK of the 'new wave' style that gained such recognition in California. Her previous books include *A Feast of Flavours*, *Evergreen: Classic Vegetarian Cookery* and *Not-So-Wicked Puddings*.

MORE TASTE THAN TIME

Annie Bell

EBURY PRESS
London

DEDICATION
For Simon Slingsby

First published in 1996

Text © Annie Bell 1996
Cover photographs by Jean Cazals © Ebury Press 1996

First published in the United Kingdom in 1996 by Ebury Press
Random House, 20 Vauxhall Bridge Road, London SW1V 2SA

Random House Australia (Pty) Limited
20 Alfred Street, Milsons Point, Sydney,
New South Wales 2061, Australia

Random House New Zealand Limited
187 Poland Road, Glenfield, Auckland 10, New Zealand

Random House South Africa (Pty) Limited
PO Box 337, Bergvlei, South Africa

Random House UK Limited Reg. No. 954009

A CIP catalogue record for this book is available from the British Library.

ISBN   978 009 1949 945

Text typeset and designed by Bob Vickers
Cover design by the Senate
Cover photography by Jean Cazals

The Random House Group Limited supports The Forest Stewardship Council® (FSC®), the leading international forest-certification organisation. Our books carrying the FSC label are printed on FSC®-certified paper. FSC is the only forest-certification scheme supported by the leading environmental organisations, including Greenpeace. Our paper procurement policy can be found at www.randomhouse.co.uk/environment

MIX
Paper from
responsible sources
FSC® C018072

Printed and bound in Great Britain by Clays Ltd, St Ives plc

CONTENTS

NOTES

All spoons are level unless otherwise stated

Oven temperatures: the fan oven temperature is given first, then the temperatures for non-fan electric ovens and gas ovens

Egg sizing: size 2 corresponds to a large egg

PREFACE

HOW FAST IS FAST?

'Fast' is like a disease that has crept through the media: if you can't cook fast, don't cook at all. It is my belief that we are way out of control on this issue, because a lot of what is good to eat and pleasurable to cook is being squeezed by a stop-watch, or otherwise ignored. And much that calls itself fast resides in a grey area. Fast assumes that it can be done in 30 minutes. Well, one person's 30 minutes is another person's 50 minutes. Does it include the washing up? You can go hell for leather during 30 minutes and build up a double sink load of pans that take another 30 minutes to clean.

So I have not stuck to any rigid 30-minute rules – these are recipes that I believe are possible to produce without too much sweat. I have also included a handful of slow-cook dishes that don't require much in the way of preparation, because it seems nonsensical to exclude something that takes 10 minutes to assemble just because it then takes an hour in the oven, or because one ingredient may require soaking or resting; these recipes are marked with a *. However, desserts that require chilling are not marked, as they are usually made in advance of eating.

INTRODUCTION

More Taste than Time is a response to a modern dilemma – the need to entertain, when you haven't got the time – which I suffer from every bit as much as you. The recipes in this book are ones I turn to, confident that they are special enough for friends, without being overly complex. They are based on my time spent as *Vogue*'s cookery writer, and as such reflect today's manner of cooking and eating.

In retrospect, conquering outer space seems a doddle compared to solving the problem of entertaining. Just about everything has been tried in the name of convenience and speed, be it desiccated or frozen, cooked, chilled or bottled, and none of it comes anywhere close to the real thing.

It was moving house recently that brought home to me the extent of this reality. There was no time to cook; it was just packing, shifting, unpacking, over and over. And in any case the kitchen was in no fit state to receive ingredients. To begin with it felt like a holiday from the stove.

The first takeaway from our new local was pretty good, and during the fortnight that followed we worked our way through supermarket convenience food. But the longer it went on the worse it became until eventually my husband said words to the effect of 'I can't stand this any longer', by arriving home with the wherewithal to cook himself supper.

The truth that gradually dawned was that however spicy the food purported to be, none of it tasted of anything. Rarely did it taste fresh, and worst of all you never felt satisfied afterwards. Whatever place such convenience does have, it does not, I'm afraid, extend to entertaining. There is only one solution for it: roll up your sleeves and start cooking.

The good news is that it has never been easier to entertain with greater style or greater speed. You are probably tired of cookery writers banging on about raw materials, but we do have access to an incredible range of fresh produce from all over the world. Added to this we have most fresh vegetables and fruit all year round. Having said that, I like my asparagus and strawberries in season; however, I also recognise the advantages of being able to supplement the seasonal supply with out-of-season produce at one's whim.

The second strand to this is the availability of high quality storecupboard ingredients such as olive oils and vinegars, olives and canned anchovies, saffron filaments, harissa, mustards and so forth: very little has to be done to fresh produce in order to produce something that looks and tastes wonderful.

All this is not to say we have gone 'grunge' on food. In fact, it has never been more glamorous, but today it is a quiet, understated glamour that says 'I know how to shop properly', rather than 'I spent the whole of yesterday cooking'.

When I think of yesterday's party piece I think of a whole poached salmon, skinned and presented with a decorative line of cucumber slices and mayonnaise piped in swirls up and down its length (though this one still has a habit of cropping up, usually overcooked, at weddings and special occasions, followed by strawberries and cream). A thoroughly modern fish would be a whole roasted seabass, smothered with extra virgin olive oil, lots of freshly chopped herbs and finely grated lemon zest, and a splash of balsamic vinegar, the dressing warmed through in the roasting pan with the fish juices, and poured over.

It must be a dilemma for cooks that food writers hop from one continent to another, apparently without thinking about it. There again, as professionals it is only right that they can with some ease cook Italian one day, Thai the next and Moroccan the day after. The chances are that you don't cook like that.

If I look around my friends who are keen cooks, or who entertain a lot, most of them will have one type of cooking they are good at and enjoy doing, be it Vietnamese, Italian or Mexican. They will also have a repertoire of dishes that they know work well and are confident of producing at a party.

The influences within this particular collection of recipes are very varied, as they have been collected from trips all over the world during my time at Vogue. For myself, the greatest gratification is not that you should want to try one or all of them, but that if you do try any of them that you should want to cook it again.

SHOPPING

Perfect food shopping means being within easy shopping reach of a good butcher, fishmonger and greengrocer, a bread shop, a cheese shop and a couple of foreign delis: an Italian and one specialising in Far Eastern food should see you through. And, of course, a supermarket.

I confess to being fortunate in West London where I do have access to all these shops; and if all else fails then there are the department stores which carry a pretty cosmopolitan range of ingredients. But I am very aware that there are areas of the country which for no explicable reason are like culinary deserts.

There has been a big increase in recent years in mail order services, and this is something to consider if you are a keen cook and disappointed with what you have locally. Henrietta Green's Food Lovers' Guide to Britain (BBC Books) is an excellent reference book to assist in sourcing ingredients, shops and mail order services, and it is regularly updated.

The last few years has also seen the growth of organic box schemes, which have done a transatlantic hop from the U.S.A. They are an excellent way of acquiring fresh, local organic produce. The idea is that a farmer supplies you regularly with about ten different vegetables and sometimes fruit, depending on what he is growing. Normally, you do not know in advance what you will get, which can make planning parties tricky. But it is a scheme worth looking into. The Soil Association produces a booklet listing local schemes called 'Local Food Links' (available from 86 Colston Street, Bristol BS1 5BB, tel. 01179 290661).

BREAKFAST AND BRUNCH

'Breakfast like a king, lunch like a prince and supper like a pauper' is advice handed out to those wanting to keep their figures trim. Eminently sensible advice. It is amazing what you can get away with at breakfast-time if you behave yourself for the rest of the day.

The main point about breakfast is that we need it – it is the fuel our body requires as we break our fast from the night before. But to see it simply in terms of fuel one might as well resort to some vitamin-enhanced breakfast cereal that is on a par with dog biscuits with milk.

Whether you choose to break your fast as soon as you get up, or later in the morning, your palate is at its freshest and most sensitive, and there is every reason for being choosy about what morsels pass your lips.

While on our honeymoon in Tobago my husband and I stayed in an idyllic house overlooking the sea, surrounded by bountiful avocados and mangoes. First thing every morning the longtime retainer, called Shadow, would make his way slowly up the drive accompanied by a posse of stray dogs, a hessian sack slung over his shoulder. He would deposit a prize papaya, almost the size of a watermelon, on the table on the veranda, and we would slice it and squeeze a lime over. I think this remains my all-time favourite instant breakfast. And if it isn't that, then it's some Greek yoghurt with a spoonful of runny honey, plus some fresh berries during the summer.

On the rare occasions I stay in a swanky country house hotel, the greatest luxury is the little tray of early morning tea with home-made biscuits that arrives with a quiet knock on the door, just as you are waking up – enough to fuel you through to getting up and maybe going for a stroll, so that you can build up a bit of an appetite and do justice to a more serious breakfast or brunch later on.

I do know people who fervently object to the notion of brunch – they feel robbed of a meal since two are rolled into one. But for those like myself, who do not have much appetite first thing, it is perfect: a late breakfast would spoil your lunch, so a really hearty meal that rolls all the best aspects of breakfast and lunch into one is the answer.

Brunch is the time I want to eat salty Stilton and tomato rarebits on granary toast; a fry-up of pumpkin, peppers and eggs; or a smoky kedgeree; or to dip asparagus spears into a soft boiled egg, or eat an Omelette Arnold Bennett. For that matter, I could cope with some *pain perdu* made with panettone, eaten with a jammy bowl of plum compote, or some of those little fried Spanish doughnuts called *churros*, dipped into a thick hot chocolate.

While comparatively quick, these things do require more time to prepare than you are likely to have before rushing off to work, which is why it is such a treat at the weekend to make a big thing of brunch, with lots of newspapers, a large jug of Bloody Mary and some good coffee.

There is one final reason why I am so fond of this meal: it gives me an excuse to eat a variety of foods that I love which don't seem to fit into any other mealtime. On a hot day it would be croissants filled with strawberries and vanilla ice-cream, and on a cold one a bowl of oatmeal porridge with a slop of whisky and lots of brown sugar and cream.

FRUIT DISHES AND CEREAL

Fresh Figs with Ricotta, Honey and Almonds

Serves 4

My husband walked in one August morning with a pile of figs he had just picked from a tree in a friend's garden – in fact, it had only been planted that year. I always think of figs in Mediterranean terms and forget how well they do on native soil.

You can buy toasted flaked almonds, and these make a useful addition to the storecupboard, although there is quite a difference from freshly toasted almonds which have that squeaky crispness. To toast almonds, spread them on a baking sheet and toast in a preheated 170°C (fan oven)/180°C (350°F) gas 4 oven for 8–10 minutes until lightly golden.

---

250 g (9 oz) fresh figs, or 1 per person
4 tablespoons ricotta

8 teaspoons clear honey
2 heaped tablespoons flaked almonds, toasted

Trim the top of the figs and quarter them. Place the quarters in the centre of 4 small plates. On top place a tablespoon of ricotta. Drizzle the honey over and scatter with almonds.

Papaya and Lime

I am not sure that this requires a recipe any more than avocado vinaigrette does. This is more to remind you of that perfumed, delectably sweet orange flesh that melts in your mouth to a rich purée, sharpened with lime. One of nature's great combinations.

Papayas come in sizes ranging from a pear to a football: select ones larger than a pear, about twice the size; they should yield to the pressure of your thumb. Slice them in half lengthwise and scoop out the seeds and membrane. Serve with wedges of lime to squeeze over as you eat.

You could, of course, make life totally effortless for your guests by first cutting the skin off the papaya, then slicing it open lengthwise and scooping out the seeds, and finally cutting into thin slivers.

Pear with Raspberry Compote and Greek Yoghurt

Serves 6

Pears are poached in a spiced syrup and chilled overnight, and the raspberries are added the following morning.

It is essential that the chilli is whole and unbroken – the chilli provides a mild heat and an aroma, and if the seeds and membranes were in any way exposed the result would be disastrous. So if in doubt leave it out.

---

300 ml (½ pint) white wine	15 saffron filaments
300 ml (½ pint) water	1 red chilli
175 g (6 oz) caster sugar	900 g (2 lb) pears
3 sprigs fresh thyme	225 g (8 oz) raspberries
3 bay leaves	
1 length of lemon grass, halved	To serve
lengthwise	Greek yoghurt

Place the wine, water, sugar, herbs, saffron filaments and chilli in a medium-size saucepan, bring to a simmer, cover and cook for 15 minutes. Remove and discard the chilli.

While the syrup is simmering, peel the pears. Poach them in the syrup for 15 minutes or until tender, turning them over halfway through. Remove to a bowl. The remaining syrup should be viscous, so reduce it further if necessary. Pour the syrup over the fruit, leaving in the herbs. Once cool, cover and chill.

Just before serving, remove and discard the herbs, and stir in the raspberries. You can slice the pears off their cores before serving if you like. Eat with plenty of Greek yoghurt.

Melon filled with Raspberries and Passionfruit

Serves 4

The perfect hot-weather start to the day and beautiful to behold. If you happen to have some fruit eau-de-vie, just a splash will enliven it.

The success of this medley does depend on the sweetness of the fruit – beware of tart passionfruit seeds – although you can always sprinkle some sugar over the nectarine and raspberries. I have suggested Charentais melons, but most melons will do.

---

2 Charentais melons, about 900 g (2 lb) each	250 g (9 oz) raspberries
1 white nectarine or peach	2 passionfruit

Cut a thin slice off the top and bottom of each melon to prevent it rolling on the plate; halve and scoop out the seeds. Halve the nectarine or peach, remove the stone and slice into crescents. Mix the raspberries and nectarine in a bowl and fill the melon cavities so they are piled high. Halve the passionfruit and spoon the seeds over the fruit in the centre.

Pink Grapefruit grilled with Muscovado Sugar

Serves 4

Muscovado has that lovely treacley flavour that goes especially well with the grapefruit, but you can use any brown sugar.

---

4 pink grapefruits
4 dessertspoons muscovado sugar

First slice the skin and pith off the grapefruits, then run a knife between the segments to remove them. Place the segments neatly in a circle on 4 heatproof plates, or in an ovenproof dish, with a couple of segments in the centre. Preheat the grill. Sprinkle the sugar over the grapefruit and place under the grill until the fruit is warm and the sugar melted.

Oatmeal Porridge with Whisky

Serves 4

The best porridge splutters away like a quagmire of mud for a good 20 minutes before you smother it with sugar, cream and a generous shot of whisky.

For the porridge
225 g (8 oz) medium oatmeal
1.2 litres (2 pints) water
1/2 teaspoon sea salt

To serve
8 heaped teaspoons soft
  brown, muscovado or vanilla
  sugar
4 tablespoons whisky
4 tablespoons double cream

Place the oatmeal, water and salt in a saucepan and bring to the boil over a high heat, stirring constantly. Turn the heat to low and continue to cook for 25 minutes until the oatmeal is swollen and thick; stir occasionally.

Serve in bowls at the table, with the sugar, whisky and cream served separately.

Mia's Muesli*

Serves 4

Mia, who was our Swiss au pair when I was young, made quite the best muesli I have ever tasted. And it bore no relation whatsoever to the desiccated packet varieties crammed with indigestibility.

The night before, she would put some oatmeal on to soak in milk, and the following morning, when it was thick, swollen and gloopy, she would stir in lots of double cream (use yoghurt if you are feeling virtuous). We would eat it with fresh fruit and toasted nuts scattered over the top.

Ready toasted and chopped hazelnuts are useful to have in the storecupboard, but to prepare them freshly, heat the oven to 170°C (fan oven)/180°C (350°F) gas 4 and toast the hazelnuts on a tray for 8–10 minutes until lightly coloured. Cool and then chop them.

---

250 g (9 oz) medium oatmeal
2 rounded tablespoons soft
  brown sugar
400 ml (14 fl oz) milk
2 figs
1 large banana

4 tablespoons double cream
ground cinnamon
115 g (4 oz) seedless grapes
1 heaped tablespoon toasted
  and chopped hazelnuts

Place the oatmeal and sugar in a bowl, stir in the milk, cover and leave in the fridge overnight.

To serve, cut the figs into thin slivers and slice the banana. Pour off any liquid sitting on the surface of the oatmeal, stir it well and add the cream. Spoon into 4 cereal bowls, dust with cinnamon and scatter over the fruit and hazelnuts.

SWEET BREADS

Cinnamon Toast and Rhubarb Compote*

Serves 4

Cinnamon toast may seem rich for this time of the day, but it is pleasantly masked by the tartness of the fruit. There is a point where the sugar melts and the toast becomes cloaked in toffee; stop just short of this, when the sugar has fused with the butter and is bubbling, but not molten.

Forced rhubarb is one of the only fruits to brave very cold weather early in the year, baby pink stems that do not require peeling. Any jam can be used for the compote, but quince jelly and other fragrant jams are a good choice.

---

1 cinnamon stick
25 g (1 oz) caster sugar
4 slices day-old white bread,
   crusts removed
unsalted butter

For the compote
675 g (1½ lb) forced rhubarb
   (untrimmed weight)
225 g (8 oz) jam or jelly (see
   above)

To make the compote, cut the rhubarb into pieces and layer in a baking dish with jam (first work the jam and sieve it until it is smooth). Cover with foil and bake at 180°C (fan oven)/190°C (375°F) gas 5 for 45 minutes. The pieces of rhubarb should remain whole, and the juices from the fruit will combine with the melted jam to make a delicious syrup. You can always sweeten it with sugar to taste.

Break up the cinnamon stick and reduce to a powder in an electric grinder; mix 1 heaped teaspoon with the caster sugar.

Preheat the grill. Toast the bread on both sides. Butter one side and sprinkle 1 or 2 heaped teaspoons of cinnamon sugar over. Put back under the grill until it just starts to melt. Cut the toast into quarters and serve with the compote, which can be warm or at room temperature, but not boiling hot.

Welsh Cakes, or *pice ar y maen**

Makes 14

This is a home speciality that no professional baker is likely to improve upon. They are part of our British legacy of sweet, spicy breads.

Welsh cakes resemble thin scones and are cooked on a griddle, though a cast-iron frying pan is just as good. This recipe comes from my great-grandmother-in-law, of Welsh valley stock. Crisp on the outside, the scones are flavoured with mace and studded with currants, split while hot and spread with lots of melted butter and jam.

---

350 g (12 oz) plain flour
1/2 teaspoon sea salt
1 teaspoon baking powder
3/4 teaspoon freshly ground
    mace
175 g (6 oz) unsalted butter,
    chilled and diced

115 g (4 oz) caster sugar
115 g (4 oz) currants
1 egg (size 2), beaten
milk
lard or clarified butter for
    cooking

Place the flour, salt, baking powder and mace in a bowl and rub in the butter with your hands until the mixture is crumb-like. Mix in the sugar and currants and then the egg to bring the dough together. A little milk can be added if necessary. Wrap in clingfilm and rest for 30 minutes in the fridge, though the dough will keep overnight.

Roll out the dough 5 mm (1/4 inch) thick on a floured surface and cut into 7.5 cm (3 inch) rounds with a fluted cutter. Gather up the trimmings and roll out to cut more rounds (only roll twice). Grease a griddle or cast-iron frying pan with lard or clarified butter and heat, then cook the scones for 3 minutes on each side or until they are mottled brown. Slice while hot and spread with butter and jam.

Cape Gooseberry Muffins

Makes 14

Muffins warm from the oven, domed and golden, are something Americans know best: 'the missing link between cake and bread' is how Beth Hensperger describes them in her book *Bread*. Use this recipe as the basis for whatever ingredient takes your fancy, be it dates, Cape gooseberries and banana, raspberries, or pecans and chocolate.

This method of making the muffins, where the butter and sugar are creamed together, produces a cake-like muffin that will last the day and still be delicious.

---

115 g (4 oz) unsalted butter
115 g (4 oz) caster sugar
2 eggs (size 2)
1 teaspoon pure vanilla
   essence
225 g (8 oz) plain flour
2 teaspoons baking powder
1/4 teaspoon salt
125 ml (4 fl oz) milk

85 g (3 oz) banana, mashed
   (weight excluding skin)
140 g (5 oz) Cape goose-
   berries, chopped (weight
   excluding husk)
3 teaspoons caster sugar
   mixed with 1/2 teaspoon
   freshly grated nutmeg

Preheat the oven to 200°C (fan oven)/220°C (425°F) gas 7. Butter the muffin moulds, which should have steep sides and a flat base.

Beat the butter and sugar in a food processor until pale and fluffy. Incorporate the eggs and vanilla essence. Transfer the creamed mixture to a bowl. Sift together the flour, baking powder and salt, and very gently work half this and half the milk into the creamed mixture. Then mix in the remaining dry ingredients and milk, together with the fruit. Spoon the batter into the muffin moulds, sprinkle with a little nutmeg sugar and bake for approximately 17 minutes.

Loosen the muffins with a knife and turn on to a wire rack to cool for 10 minutes before eating.

Churros y Chocos

Serves 4

In Seville, come Semana Santa, Feria, New Year or for that matter any Saturday night when the tired habitués of the flamenco bars spill out on to the streets at dawn, Sevillians will make for the nearest bar or stall selling *churros y chocos*.

Churros y chocos are the original Dunkin' Donuts. The dough, made simply from flour and water, is piped through a fluted nozzle; it can be shaped as a horseshoe, or more festively as a large, curled length. The churros are cooked in a giant cauldron of hot oil and broken up once cooked, to be eaten with hot chocolate, dipped into it piece by piece. At breakfast the chocolate is usually a rich drink, but at other times it resembles a thin sauce and the churros are eaten as a dessert.

This is wickedly rich and defies every guideline on cholesterol. Certainly as a national breakfast, it belies the slender and graceful forms of most Sevillians. Perhaps they work it off in the flamenco bars.

A *churrera* is a specially designed instrument for piping the dough, but a piping bag with a star-shaped nozzle 1 cm (½ inch) in diameter can be used. The churros can be piped in advance and stored between layers of baking parchment or clingfilm for several hours. Pipe the dough into 10-cm (4-inch) lengths or equivalent shapes.

This recipe comes from *The Festive Food of Spain* by Nicholas Butcher.

---

500 ml (18 fl oz) water	To serve
275 g (9½ oz) plain flour	Hot Chocolate (see below)
½ teaspoon salt	
a tasteless oil for deep-frying	

Boil the water in a saucepan, then add the sifted flour and salt and work to a smooth, thick paste. Cook for a couple of minutes. Remove and cool, then pipe (see above).

Deep-fry the churros in hot oil until golden and crisp. Drain on kitchen paper. Serve immediately with hot chocolate.

Hot Chocolate

Serves 4

Warm, thick and luxuriant, this is to be taken in small draughts, dipping the churros into it as you go.

---

450 ml (¾ pint) full-cream milk	85 g (3 oz) dark chocolate
2 cm (¾ inch) cinnamon stick	50 ml (2 fl oz) double cream
25 g (1 oz) milk chocolate	

Place the milk in a saucepan, crumble in the cinnamon stick and bring to the boil; remove from the heat and infuse for 15 minutes.

To melt the chocolate, chop it into small pieces and place in a bowl over simmering water. Do not rush it: periodically remove the bowl from the water and let the retained warmth continue to melt the chocolate. Stir in the cream.

Strain the milk, reheat and whisk gradually into the chocolate mixture. Serve in small cups.

Jean-Christophe Novelli's Pain Perdu

Serves 6

The memory of his mother's *pain perdu* has Jean-Christophe Novelli, of Maison Novelli, eulogising 'I nearly die'. It is, as he puts it, 'a proletarian pudding', but typically his is not just any old *pain perdu*: it is caramelised with the help of a little honey, flambéed with kirsch and served hot with a vanilla ice-cream melting over it. Strictly French, Jean-Christophe uses brioche, but an obvious ploy is to use panettone. And if the ice-cream seems too rich for mid-morning you could always go for a large dollop of Greek yoghurt and a little honey.

---

2 eggs (size 2)
150 ml (¼ pint) milk
55 g (2 oz) caster sugar
115 g (4 oz) unsalted butter,
    clarified
clear honey for frying
6 large slices of brioche or
    panettone

1–2 tablespoons kirsch or marc
    de Champagne

To serve
vanilla ice-cream

Whisk the eggs, milk and sugar together in a shallow bowl. Using two frying pans at once, heat a little clarified butter with 1 teaspoon of honey in each one. If the slices of brioche or panettone are large, cut them in half. Dip both sides in the egg and milk mixture, then fry over a moderate heat until coloured and caramelised around the edges. Lay out on one or two serving plates. Scrape out the pans and cook the remainder of the brioche or panettone in the same way.

Heat the alcohol in a ladle over a flame, ignite and pour it over the pain perdu. Serve immediately, with some ice-cream on top.

Croissants with Pistachio Paste

Serves 4–6

I ate something similar to this created by Le Baumanière in Provence. It is wonderfully exotic and luxurious and, as you will see, could not be easier to prepare yourself.

6 croissants	3 tablespoons clear honey
	2 tablespoons amaretto
For the pistachio paste	liqueur
175 g (6 oz) shelled pistachio	4 tablespoons boiling water
nuts (unsalted)	pinch of salt

Place all the ingredients for the pistachio paste in a food processor and reduce to a sticky, fine-grained paste – it will be very thick. Serve with the croissants.

Panettone and Cinnamon-Kirsch Butter

Serves 4

This is decadent wintertime stuff, and any fruited bread will do.

6–8 large slices of panettone	25 g (1 oz) icing sugar, sifted
	½ teaspoon ground cinnamon
For the cinnamon-kirsch butter	1 tablespoon kirsch or dark
85 g (3 oz) unsalted butter	rum

Cut the butter into small pieces and blend in a food processor with the sugar and cinnamon. Incorporate the kirsch a little at a time.

Preheat the grill. Toast the bread on both sides under the grill and spread with the butter.

Croissants filled with Strawberries and Vanilla Ice-Cream

Serves 2

I first heard about these rolls, eaten for breakfast in the stifling heat of a Sicilian summer morning, while on a trip to Palermo – unfortunately I was there at the wrong time of year. But it still seemed to me to be the most magical breakfast, and the croissants are fabulously delicious.

---

2 croissants	85 g (3 oz) strawberries, hulled
4 tablespoons vanilla	and sliced
ice-cream	

Slit the croissants in half, spread the ice-cream over the base and scatter the strawberries on top. Close and serve straightaway.

SAVOURY ROLLS AND TOASTS

Toasted Sandwich of Grilled Tuna and Black Pepper Boursin

Serves 2

Black pepper Boursin is one of those classic great conveniences. As a teenager I had a boyfriend whose star-turn in the kitchen was steak grilled with Boursin. I was frightfully impressed.

---

15 cm (6 inch) length of ciabatta	sea salt and black pepper
225 g (8 oz) fresh tuna, sliced 1 cm (½ inch) thick, skin removed	unsalted butter 85 g (3 oz) black pepper Boursin
extra virgin olive oil	1 medium-size tomato, sliced

Preheat an overhead grill and a griddle or ridged cast-iron grill pan. Slit the ciabatta open lengthwise. Cut the tuna into two steaks, brush with olive oil and season them. Cook the tuna on the griddle or grill pan for about 3 minutes total, turning once. (I like it pink in the centre, so if you prefer it better done cook it for longer.)

Grill the bread on both sides at the same time as you are cooking the tuna. Butter the bread and spread the Boursin on the bottom half. Lay the tuna on top, arrange the tomato slices on top of this, close and serve straightaway.

Lewis Scallop Rolls

On the Isle of Lewis in the Outer Hebrides, if you're still up and feeling game at 1 am, you can wander down to the quayside in Stornoway and haggle with the fishermen as they trade their catch. Or you can wait until morning and buy it from the local fish shop as we did, walking off with a bag full of scallops. We found a remote beach with white sand and piercingly blue water, lit a fire and pan-fried them. As we were unable to wash out the pan, each successive batch caramelised with greater speed. Tipped hot with their juices on to buttered rolls, they made a scallop sandwich from heaven.

Stilton and Tomato Rarebit

Stilton and tomato rarebits are manna during those days following Christmas when it is cold and generally horrible outside, and you have been given a whole Stilton and are running out of ideas of how to use it.

Stilton is not a hardy, long-living cheese. Once it has ripened to the consistency of butter right the way through, creamy and marbled with a restrained number of veins that are the colour of green lichen, tinged with yellow and hints of blue, then it should be eaten within a week.

Stilton makes a mean rarebit: toast some walnut or wholegrain bread, underlay slices of Stilton with a few thin slices of tomato and give it a quick blast under a hot grill followed by a dusting of cayenne pepper, and serve straightaway.

Smoked Salmon and Watercress Bagels

Serves 2

3 bagels	lemon juice
unsalted butter	black pepper
115 g (4 oz) smoked salmon	55 g (2 oz) watercress

Slit and butter the bagels. Lay the smoked salmon inside and season it with lemon juice and pepper, then place masses of watercress on top. Close the bagels so the watercress and salmon are spilling out at the sides.

Crumpets with Creamed Mushrooms

Serves 2

With all the attention poured on newly arrived breads, it is easy to overlook those that have been around for some time, such as crumpets. Toasted and dripping in butter, they are quite superb smothered with a pile of shiitake mushrooms.

25 g (1 oz) unsalted butter, and more for buttering the crumpets	85 ml (3 fl oz) double cream
200 g (7 oz) shiitake mushrooms, sliced	1/2 teaspoon finely chopped fresh tarragon, or 2 level teaspoons finely chopped fresh chervil
sea salt and black pepper	2 crumpets
50 ml (2 fl oz) white wine	

Melt the butter in a frying pan, add the mushrooms and cook until they become limp, seasoning them. Add the wine and cook to evaporate it, then add the cream and cook until the mushrooms are coated in a thick sauce. Stir in the herbs.

Toast the crumpets on both sides, butter them and pile the mushrooms on top.

Croissants with Parma Ham and Avocado

Serves 2

I also like these with the addition of fontina cheese, so if you happen to be buying your ham in an Italian deli you could buy some fontina as well.

---

2 croissants
85 g (3 oz) Parma ham, or other
  air-dried ham

½ avocado
lemon juice
black pepper

Slice open the croissants and fill with Parma ham. (You can do this in advance.) Just before serving, peel the avocado by incising the skin into quarters; remove the flesh in two halves and slice. Place this on top of the ham and season with lemon juice and pepper.

Anchovy and Goat's Cheese Molletes

Molletes are small, oval shaped rolls, typically served in Sevillian tapas bars morning, noon and night. They may be filled with cured meats, or anchovies, or a soft goat's cheese and spicy peppers – the combinations are endless.

To prepare a mollete preheat the grill. Halve a small, soft white roll and dribble a little olive oil on the cut surfaces. Place a couple of slices of goat's cheese and a salted anchovy or two in the centre. Close the roll and place it under the grill for a couple of minutes, turning it as the top starts to brown, so as to toast the base. The mollete should be warm and crisp on the outside, with the cheese just heated through but not melted.

EGGS

Shirred Eggs with Tarragon Butter

Serves 2

What a sensible way of cooking eggs, half-fried and then glazed under the grill, so you get that perfect combination of nicely set base and a runny yolk. You can serve these with toast, mushrooms or whatever else you are having.

---

25 g (1 oz) unsalted butter, diced
1 heaped teaspoon finely chopped fresh tarragon

sea salt and black pepper
squeeze of lemon juice
4 eggs (size 2)

Preheat the grill. Blend the butter with the tarragon and seasoning, and mix in the lemon juice. Spread half the butter on the base of a shallow flameproof dish (I use a casserole lid) and break the eggs into it. Season them and dot with the remaining tarragon butter.

Cook the eggs on the hob until the base has a thin layer of cooked white. Place under the grill until the white and the yolks appear set on the surface. This all happens very quickly, so watch carefully.

Omelette Arnold Bennett

Serves 2

Arnold Bennett was a frequent visitor to the Savoy, hence the origins of this omelette, a fantastic creation of goo: unset egg blending with melted cheese and creamy haddock, it just sort of oozes.

---

175 g (6 oz) smoked haddock, ideally Finnan	sea salt and black pepper
1 bay leaf	pinch of cayenne pepper
200 ml (7 fl oz) milk	85 ml (3 fl oz) whipping cream
15 g (½ oz) unsalted butter	5 eggs (size 2)
15 g (½ oz) plain flour, less 1 teaspoon	2 teaspoons vegetable oil
	55 g (2 oz) grated Gruyère

Place the haddock and bay leaf in a small saucepan and cover with the milk. Bring to the boil, half cover the saucepan and poach for 5 minutes. Remove the fish and flake it; reserve the milk.

Melt the butter in the saucepan, add the flour and cook this roux for a minute or two. Gradually blend in the milk, return to the heat and bring to the boil, stirring. Simmer for 5 minutes over a low heat, stirring occasionally. Add the fish and seasonings.

Preheat the grill. Whip the cream until it is stiff. Break the eggs into a bowl and whisk lightly. Heat the oil in a 25 cm (10 inch) frying pan with an 18 cm (7 inch) base; when it appears very hot, tip out the excess oil. Add the eggs and scramble rapidly for 30 seconds until almost set; allow another 30 seconds for the base to set.

Quickly fold the whipped cream into the hot haddock mixture, spoon it over the omelette and scatter over the cheese. Place under the grill until the cheese is melted and bubbling, and serve straightaway.

Soft Boiled Eggs with Asparagus Soldiers

Serves 2

Does anyone ever grow too old for the elementary act of dipping something into a runny egg yolk? If anything, it's what you dip that changes as you get older – toast when you're five, asparagus when you're older. You might like some brown bread and butter with this one as well.

350 g (12 oz) finger-thick asparagus	sea salt and black pepper
4 eggs (size 2)	2 teaspoons freshly grated Parmesan
15 g (½ oz) unsalted butter	

Trim the asparagus spears at the point where they appear to become woody, and peel to within 2.5 cm (1 inch) of the tip. Bring a large pan of water to the boil and cook the asparagus and eggs together, giving the asparagus 5 minutes and the eggs 4 minutes.

Remove asparagus and toss with the butter and seasoning. Place on two plates and scatter over the Parmesan. Serve the eggs in cups beside the asparagus, with more salt and pepper for seasoning them as you go.

Ivan's Feta and Mint Frittata

Serves 2–3

I vaguely know who Ivan is, but I know his omelette better: this frittata has been doing the rounds amongst my friends. I think the reason it is so popular is that it can be produced in double-quick time, and it is one of those unlikely but highly successful combinations.

---

6 eggs (size 2)
2 tablespoons double cream
sea salt and black pepper
extra virgin olive oil

85 g (3 oz) feta, crumbled
1 heaped tablespoon chopped
   fresh mint

Beat the eggs with the cream and seasoning in a bowl. Preheat the grill. Heat a little olive oil in a 20 cm (8 inch) frying pan until it is very hot, then tip out the excess. Add the eggs and scramble until they are semi-set; cook for a minute longer to set the base. Scatter the feta and mint over, pressing them down into the omelette. Place under the grill for about 1 minute until the top is set. The cheese should be soft and the omelette remain slightly baveuse in the centre. Serve it in wedges.

Huevos Revueltos

Serves 2

Huevos revueltos is Spanish for scrambled eggs, but they do it differently. More like a scrambled omelette, it might include broad beans, mushrooms, peppers, peas, artichokes, asparagus or thin strips of ham, all of which are added in high proportion to the eggs, unlike a traditional omelette which is mainly egg with a modicum of filling.

Like all the best egg dishes, *revueltos* is versatile and can be used simply as a vessel for using up odds and ends, or made into an exotic dish with wild mushrooms and truffles. This recipe feeds two people; if increasing the quantity, make in two lots or use a larger pan.

---

1 small red pepper, peeled, cored and deseeded
2 tablespoons extra virgin olive oil
1 clove garlic, peeled and finely chopped

175 g (6 oz) asparagus, cooked
85 g (3 oz) peas, cooked
sea salt and black pepper
6 eggs

Cut the red pepper into strips. Heat 1 tablespoon olive oil in a frying pan and cook the red pepper and garlic until limp and tender. Add the asparagus and peas, season, and heat thoroughly (the brief cooking time of the next stage is insufficient to heat it through).

Whisk the eggs, season and combine with the vegetables. Heat the remaining olive oil in a 25 cm (10 inch) frying pan over a high heat; when it smokes tip out excess oil. Pour in the egg mixture and scramble. It will cook in about 30 seconds. Pile on to plates while still slightly moist.

FISH

Salmon Fishcakes with Lemon Butter Sauce*

Serves 4–6

Gary Rhodes, chef at The Greenhouse, features these fishcakes daily on the menu, which means they are very popular indeed. Do not worry overly about procuring wild salmon; farmed is fine.

---

675 g (1½ lb) potatoes, peeled
15 g (½ oz) unsalted butter
2 shallots, peeled and finely
    chopped
450 g (1 lb) salmon (weight
    including skin and bones)
85 ml (3 fl oz) white wine
sea salt and black pepper
1 tablespoon finely chopped
    fresh flat-leaf parsley
plain flour

1 egg, beaten
fine white breadcrumbs
groundnut oil for deep-frying

For the lemon butter sauce
225 g (8 oz) unsalted butter
juice of 1 lemon
85 ml (3 fl oz) vegetable or fish
    stock
sea salt

B oil the potatoes until tender; drain. Once surface moisture has evaporated, press the potatoes through a sieve.

Preheat the oven to 200°C (fan oven)/220°C (425°F) gas 7. Butter a shallow ovenproof dish and scatter the shallots over the bottom. Place the salmon in the dish, pour the wine over and season. Cover with foil and bake for about 12 minutes until the fish has just set; it may require longer depending on the thickness of the piece. Strain the juices into a saucepan; flake the salmon into a sieve set over the saucepan, discarding skin and bones. Press out any moisture from the salmon and reserve it in a bowl. Reduce the juices to a minimal quantity of syrupy liquid.

Mix the potato with the salmon and add the reduction, parsley and seasoning. Form into balls about 5 cm (2 inches) in diameter. Roll in flour, then egg and then breadcrumbs. Chill until required.

Heat oil in a wok or wide, shallow pan and deep-fry the fishcakes for 3–4 minutes until golden and crisp. Drain on kitchen paper and serve on a pool of sauce.

To make the sauce, place the ingredients in a small saucepan and boil together until they emulsify into a thin sauce.

Spice-fried Sardines

Serves 4

This one is ready in 10 minutes, fried until the skin is golden and spicy. Ideally, grind the spices freshly in a coffee grinder, although ready ground will do.

---

2 heaped tablespoons plain flour
2 teaspoons ground cumin
2 teaspoons ground coriander
sea salt and black pepper
4 tablespoons extra virgin olive oil

900 g (2 lb) sardines, cleaned and heads removed

To serve
lemon wedges

Blend the flour, spices and seasoning in a shallow bowl. Use two frying pans to cook the sardines: heat some olive oil in each one. Dust the sardines on all sides with the spiced flour and cook for about 3 minutes on each side. Serve with lemon wedges.

Crabcakes with a Thai Dipping Sauce

Serves 4

These are pan-Asian fishcakes, perfumed with lemon grass and coriander. They are served with a syrupy, chilli-hot liquor in which to dip them.

For the crabcakes
350 g (12 oz) white and brown crab meat, picked over
85 g (3 oz) fresh white bread-crumbs
2 spring onions, finely chopped
1 heaped tablespoon finely chopped fresh coriander
2 large fresh basil leaves, finely chopped
1 heaped teaspoon finely chopped lemon grass
2 dashes of Tabasco
1 tablespoon mayonnaise
1 egg (size 2), beaten
sea salt and black pepper
vegetable oil for shallow-frying

To coat
plain flour
1 egg, beaten
white breadcrumbs

For the dipping sauce
175 ml (6 fl oz) white wine vinegar
25 g (1 oz) caster sugar
2 large garlic cloves, peeled and finely chopped
1 teaspoon finely chopped fresh red chilli

To serve
watercress sprigs

Combine all the ingredients for the crabcakes. Shape into cakes, either 4 cm (1½ inches) in diameter for mezze size, or 6–7.5 cm (2½–3 inches) in diameter for 2 per person. Roll in flour, then egg and then breadcrumbs. Reserve, covered, in the fridge until ready to cook.

To make the sauce, simmer the vinegar with the sugar in a small saucepan until reduced by half. Place the garlic and chilli in a bowl and pour over the hot sauces. Allow to cool.

Heat 1 cm (½ inch) of oil in a frying pan and cook the fishcakes over a moderate heat for 2 minutes on each side; you can also deep-fry them. Serve with watercress sprigs and the dipping sauce.

Kedgeree

Serves 4

I have tried to return to kedgeree's slightly mysterious Indian roots by spicing it up with coriander, cumin and turmeric. Turmeric is always bought ready-ground, but I would urge you to freshly grind the coriander and cumin because the difference in flavour is significant. Salted peanuts and raisins are a part of the ritual, and some like chopped egg as well, so suit yourself.

---

25 g (1 oz) unsalted butter	125 ml (4 fl oz) milk
1 teaspoon freshly ground	125 ml (4 fl oz) double cream
coriander seeds	black pepper
1 teaspoon freshly ground	2 tablespoons coarsely
cumin seeds	chopped fresh coriander
1/4 teaspoon turmeric	
250 g (9 oz) basmati rice	To serve
1 teaspoon sea salt	lime wedges
2 Finnan smoked haddock,	roasted nuts
about 450 g (1 lb) each	raisins

Melt the butter in a medium-size saucepan. Add the spices, stir, add the rice and cook for 1 minute until it is translucent. Add 450 ml (16 fl oz) water and the salt, bring to the boil and simmer for 8 minutes. Cover with the saucepan lid, remove from the heat and leave to steam for 15 minutes.

In the meantime, put the haddock, milk, cream and black pepper in a large saucepan. Bring to a simmer, cover and cook over a moderately low heat for 5 minutes; the fish will steam. Flake the flesh, then add back to the juices in the pan and gently reheat.

Fluff the rice with a fork, stir in the haddock and juices, adjust seasoning and stir in the coriander. Serve with the lime wedges, nuts and raisins.

Smoked Salmon and Avocado Tortillas

Serves 4

Use shop-bought tortillas for this. Hass avocados, the ones with the hard, bumpy skin, have a very good nutty flavour, and because of their firm texture they slice well.

---

2 tablespoons lime juice	1–2 Hass avocados, or
sea salt	avocados of a similar size
½ teaspoon finely chopped	4 flour tortillas
fresh red chilli	225 g (8 oz) smoked salmon
2 teaspoons finely chopped red	1 tablespoon fresh coriander
onion	leaves

Season the lime juice with salt and add the chilli and onion. Peel the avocados by incising the skin into quarters and peeling it off. Now remove the flesh in two halves and cut into long slices.

Preheat the grill and toast the tortillas on both sides. Place on 4 plates, arrange the smoked salmon on top and place the avocado slices in the centre. Spoon the lime dressing over the avocado and salmon and scatter with coriander leaves. Serve straightaway.

COOKING FOR A CROWD

This is the ten plus chapter, since ten is the maximum I would want to attempt at a formally seated dinner party. It is not the size of the table that concerns me but the nature of domestic kitchens: most simply aren't set up to cater for any more than that. It boils down to room and logistics – room to lay out the dinner plates and the logistics of getting the food out hot. And if you take the other approach, that you'll dish it out at the table, you might as well be having a buffet where people will help themselves.

The main consideration is how to feed the masses without an army of staff. I habitually underestimate how much juggling is involved in producing a selection of dishes simultaneously, some of which are hot, keeping glasses filled, clearing away the dirty plates and producing the next course, clearing that away and producing coffee. And the sink, in the meantime, greets you like tomorrow's hangover. A couple of extra pairs of hands, whose job it is to wash, serve and clear, will not be idle.

But I do love this type of entertaining for the sense of occasion it offers. For one thing it gives me an excuse to dust off all those beautiful large serving vessels that rarely get an outing. It is amazing how stunning comparatively modest food can look when arranged in bountiful quantity.

I spent my early days as a cookery writer simultaneously running a catering company, and after a while settled on a certain formula which I found worked easily for anything between fifteen and fifty people. First off, I advise you to dispense with the notion of a starter and settle instead for a few rounds of appetisers with drinks beforehand. Instead, go straight to the main course, and offer up a good selection of dishes.

Plan on having a mixture of hot and cold items. Two or three hot should be suffcient, and if necessary spread the load so that one cooks in the oven and the others cook on the hob. Do remember that whatever you are cooking, if it is a sizeable quantity of food it will take considerably longer than a small amount of the same recipe. Baked potatoes are a typical horror story: you decide to bake 100 potatoes which normally take 1 hour, and there you are several hours later willing them to cook by an act of God.

Most of the recipes I give here either involve roasting in advance or cooking on the hob. Le Grand Aïoli is a glistening mass of colour: roasted pumpkin and red pepper, and whole banana shallots roasted with provençal herbs, served with a large bowl of golden aïoli. A steaming tureen of wild mushroom orzotto makes a change from risottos, and a mound of pasta, be it chilled Chinese egg noodles and white crabmeat dressed with sesame oil, or spaghetti alla carbonara, will look wonderful.

A honey-glazed ham and a roast turkey can be cooked the day before. This, too, is the advantage of tarts, especially sweet ones, which is why I have included some recipes that are not technically quick. Quick when you are dealing with numbers means not having to do it at the last minute.

In fact, desserts are easy – you can have them all made in advance. I would choose one lusciously rich chocolate pudding plus a fruit tart and a trifle or tira-mi-su, and maybe some fresh fruit. I confess that I am not a big fan of fruit salads and prefer instead the best of what is in season, served whole and unadorned.

You can also go to town on the cheeseboard. For once it is economical to buy up all those small, whole cheeses. Oatcakes and a large bunch of grapes or raisins on the vine complete the picture.

SAMPLE BUFFET MENUS

Summer

Le Grand Aïoli
Spaghetti alla Carbonara
Poached Seabass with Herbs in Oil
Saffron Potatoes
Spinach and Chickpeas
Mixed Leaves with Deep-fried Herbs and Balsamic Vinaigrette

Orange Custard Tart
Tira-mi-su with Praline and Fresh Raspberries
Grand Pot au Chocolat

Winter

Onion and Thyme Tart
Honey-glazed Ham
Prawns with Garlic
Peas and Rice
Salad of Winter Chicories, Fennel and Blood Oranges

Joel Robuchon's Plum and Almond Tart
Indian Cheesecake with Polenta Crust
Grand Pot au Chocolat

VEGETARIAN

Le Grand Aïoli*

Serves 4

I have long been enchanted by the notion of the ceremonial hat the artist Eileen Agar created for eating bouillabaisse. She might just as well have done the same for 'le grand aïoli' because it has everything to do with ceremony.

As this is a vegetarian dish I have deviated from the traditional line of vegetables with salt cod by combining boiled vegetables with ones that have been slowly roasted with thyme, rosemary and bay. Tiny Niçoise olives come into their own to provide a superb hit of flavour that salt cold otherwise provides. In the absence of these use some other black olives. Blanched samphire would be a good addition to the list of boiled vegetables if it is in season.

It is a pick 'n' mix dinner and texture is everything, combining rough with slippery, crisp or succulent and gently fibrous: fine green beans, fennel, roasted pumpkin, red pepper and banana shallots. The crowning glory is a generous dab of aïoli, a nice strong one: the mild olive oil typical of Nîmes is gentle enough for a mayonnaise, whereas most Tuscan oils would seem harsh. If unsure of the nature of an oil I find the safest bet is to combine olive oil 50–50 with groundnut oil.

For the roasted vegetables
3 large red peppers
675 g (1½ lb) pumpkin
5 banana shallots, or use large
    round ones
3 bay leaves

1 sprig fresh rosemary
4 sprigs fresh thyme
3 tablespoons extra virgin olive
    oil
sea salt and black pepper

For the boiled vegetables
2 bulbs fennel
175 g (6 oz) green beans

For the aïoli
2 egg yolks (size 2)
1 level teaspoon Dijon mustard
400–600 ml (14–16 fl oz) extra-virgin olive oil and ground-nut oil, in equal quantities

3 cloves garlic, peeled and crushed to a paste with salt
lemon juice
1 teaspoon Pernod or other pastis (optional)

To serve
115 g (4 oz) Niçoise or other black olives
slices of French bread

Preheat the oven to 170°C (fan oven)/180°C (350°F) gas 4. Remove the core and seeds from the peppers and cut into wide strips. Cut the skin off the pumpkin, remove the seeds and slice it thickly. Place these vegetables and the shallots together in a roasting dish, tuck in the herbs, pour over the olive oil and season. Roast for 1¼ hours, stirring halfway through. The edges should be nicely caramelised by the end. These vegetables should be served warm rather than hot.

You can prepare the boiled vegetables at the same time that the others are roasting. Bring a large pan of salted water to the boil. Trim the fennel bulbs, remove and discard the outer sheaves and slice into thin segments so they remain attached by the root; boil these for 15 minutes. Top and tail the beans and boil them for 3 minutes, then refresh under the cold tap.

To make the mayonnaise, whisk the egg yolks in a bowl with the mustard and gradually whisk in the oil until the emulsion is thick. Now blend in the garlic paste, lemon juice to taste and the Pernod if using.

Arrange the vegetables in separate piles on a large platter with the olives in the centre and the aïoli in a separate bowl. Accompany with the French bread.

Spaghettini with Roasted Tomato Sauce*

Serves 4

The state of our tomatoes is an on-going moan, and it is not an unfair moan either. I find the answer when they are tasteless is to roast them for a long time on a low heat to draw out their sweetness, which makes this a good sauce during winter months.

Don't be scared to serve this pasta without any further embellishment – the Italians would. If anything, serve a few langoustines or slices of lobster on top. If there are any roasting juices left in the pan, spoon these over the pasta.

---

2 kg (4½ lb) tomatoes	sea salt and black pepper
1 fresh red chilli	115 g (4 oz) shallots, peeled
5 tablespoons extra virgin olive oil	2 cloves garlic, unpeeled
1 tablespoon clear honey	280 g (10 oz) spaghettini or tagliolini

---

Preheat the oven to 160°C (fan oven)/170°C (325°F) gas 3. Cut a small cone from each tomato to remove the hard central core, then halve them. Place cut side up in a roasting tray in a single layer, with the whole chilli in the middle. Pour the olive oil and honey over and season generously. Roast for 2 hours; halfway through add the peeled shallots and garlic and baste with the juices.

Discard the chilli. Press the tomatoes through a sieve or mouli-légumes. Squeeze the garlic cloves from their skins and liquidise together with the shallots and the puréed tomatoes. Adjust the seasoning and reheat in a saucepan.

While finishing the sauce, bring a large pan of salted water to the boil. Cook the pasta, then drain, but not too dry, and toss with the tomato sauce.

Onion and Thyme Tart*

Serves 6

The consistency of the onion and thyme custard in this tart is truly exquisite, very lightly set and nice and deep, but the base can go soggy soon after it is cooked, so serve immediately.

---

250 g (9 oz) puff pastry
750 g (1 lb 10 oz) white onions
20 g (³/₄ oz) unsalted butter
1 level teaspoon sea salt
200 ml (7 fl oz) double cream
200 ml (7 fl oz) milk
2 egg yolks (size 2)

1 egg (size 2)
1 heaped tablespoon freshly
  grated Parmesan
1 teaspoon coarsely chopped
  fresh thyme
black pepper

Preheat the oven to 180°C (fan oven)/190°C (375°F) gas 5. Roll out the puff pastry 3 mm (¹/₈ inch) thick and line a 20 cm (8 inch) cake tin, 6 cm (2¹/₂ inches) deep, with a removable base. Run a rolling pin over the rim to remove the excess pastry. Prick the bottom of the pastry case with a fork and line with foil and baking beans. Bake for 25–30 minutes until lightly golden. Remove the foil and beans.

While the pastry case is baking, prepare the onions: peel, quarter and slice them. Heat the butter in a medium-size saucepan, add the onions and salt and cook, covered, over a low heat for 40 minutes, until very soft. Stir the onions occasionally to make sure they are not sticking.

In a bowl, whisk together the remaining ingredients, seasoning with pepper. Stir in the onions. Pour this filling into the baked pastry case and bake for 30–35 minutes until set and lightly golden. Allow to cool, then trim the pastry level with the filling. Serve at room temperature.

Orzotto of Pearl Barley and Wild Mushrooms*

Serves 4

I ate this at a small trattoria in Trento, in northern Italy, accompanied by *schiacciata al seme di finocchio*, a flat, circular bread, open-textured like ciabatta, studded with fennel seeds and leavened with beer. An orzotto is an inspired dish of recent origin, and porcini and pearl barley go together beautifully.

---

300 g (10½ oz) pearl barley
25 g (1 oz) dried porcini
vegetable stock
2 tablespoons extra virgin olive oil
2 cloves garlic, peeled and finely chopped

85 ml (3 fl oz) white wine
15 g (½ oz) unsalted butter
50 ml (2 fl oz) double cream
55 g (2 oz) freshly grated Parmesan
sea salt and black pepper

Soak the barley overnight in plenty of water; drain. Boil it in salted water for 15 minutes, then drain it well. Soak the porcini for 15 minutes in 300 ml (½ pint) of boiling water. Drain the porcini, reserving the liquid (discard any grit that has settled at the bottom). Make the liquid up to 600 ml (1 pint) with vegetable stock and bring to the boil.

Heat the olive oil in a saucepan and cook the garlic briefly until it gives off an aroma. Add the barley, porcini and wine and cook for a couple of minutes. Add all the boiling stock mixture and simmer for 15 minutes until it is the consistency of a risotto, stirring occasionally. Stir in the butter, cream and Parmesan and season well.

Purée of Beans with Spaghetti and Spinach*

Serves 4

I first ate this in Sicily, made with olive oil that had been pressed that day and, instead of spinach, the greens found growing wild beneath the olive trees. It is a wonderful balance of textures and a perfect backdrop for the very pungent and spicy new oil.

---

550 g (1¼ lb) dried and skinned broad beans
sea salt
85 g (3 oz) spaghetti
225 g (8 oz) young spinach leaves

extra virgin olive oil

To serve
freshly grated Parmesan

Place the broad beans in a large casserole, a clay one if possible, and cover with 2 litres (3½ pints) of water. Bring to the boil, skimming off surface foam, then cover and cook over a low heat for 3 hours, stirring occasionally – it will still be quite 'soupy' after this time. Keep an eye on the water level and add a little more as necessary. Season with salt.

Break the spaghetti into 7.5 cm (3 inch) lengths and add to the soupy purée, incorporating it gradually to prevent the strands from sticking together. Place the spinach on top of the purée. Cook covered for 5 minutes, then uncovered for 15 minutes, stirring frequently – it will firm to a spoonable mass during this time. Serve with grated Parmesan and a flask of olive oil on the table: pour a lot of oil over the beans, not just a meagre trickle.

MEAT

Tortillas with Spice-roasted Duck and Pineapple Chutney*

Serves 4

This is a play on Peking duck, a short cut being to use ready-made tortillas instead of the traditional Chinese pancakes. The real thing involves air-drying the duck – but roasted the skin is still gorgeously rich and aromatic. An average-size duck of 2–2.25 kg (4½–5 lb) will just do for four people.

The chutney finds its inspiration in a dish I ate at Postrio in San Francisco, and the spice marinade is taken from Yan-kit So's *Classic Chinese Cookbook* (Dorling Kindersley).

For the chutney
55 g (2 oz) shallots, peeled
3 cloves garlic, peeled
½ red pepper, cored and deseeded
5 mm (¼ inch) slice of root ginger, peeled and finely chopped
⅓ teaspoon finely chopped fresh red chilli
350 ml (12 fl oz) sweet white wine
175 ml (6 fl oz) white wine or Champagne vinegar
3 heaped teaspoons caster sugar
1 level teaspoon salt
400 g (14 oz) ripe pineapple (weight excluding skin), cut into 5 mm (¼ inch) dice

For the duck
2 level teaspoons five-spice powder
4 level teaspoons caster sugar
4 level teaspoons salt
2 teaspoons gin
1 x 2–2.25 kg (4½–5 lb) oven-ready duck

To serve
8–12 Mexican flour tortillas
6 spring onions, trimmed and cut into fine 7.5 cm (3 inch) strips
175 g (6 oz) cucumber, peeled, deseeded and cut into fine 7.5 cm (3 inch) strips

To make the chutney, finely dice the shallots, garlic and red pepper and place in a small saucepan with the ginger, chilli, wine, vinegar, sugar and salt. Put the pineapple in a sieve set in a bowl and press to release some of the juice. Add the juice to the pan. Bring the contents of the pan to the boil and cook until the liquor is thick and syrupy, about 30–35 minutes. Stir in the pineapple, then remove the chutney to a bowl to cool.

While the chutney is cooking, prepare the duck. Preheat the oven to 180°C (fan oven)/190°C (375°F) gas 5. Blend the spice, sugar and salt with the gin, and smear inside the duck and all over the skin. Roast the duck on a rack, breast side up, for 20 minutes, then turn it over using two spoons to avoid piercing the skin and roast for a further 25 minutes. Turn it breast side up again and roast for another 20–25 minutes. Allow it to rest for 10 minutes out of the oven. Carve the skin off, then slice the flesh.

While the duck is resting, warm the tortillas in the oven, covered with foil. Allow each person to assemble their own tortilla by placing some duck skin and flesh in the centre, then some chutney and a few strips of onions and cucumber, before rolling it up.

Roast Turkey with Spinach, Apricot and Pine Nut Stuffing*

Serves 8–10

Don't think that you have to save turkey for Christmas dinner, because it is excellent buffet material, hot or cold, and as you know from experience it goes an awfully long way.

This is an Ian McAndrew-inspired stuffing. The spinach and apricots offer succulence, and as it absorbs the bird's juices the stuffing acquires a lovely consistency. Be sure to cook your stuffing inside the bird; cooking it separately defeats the object.

---

1 x 5.4 kg (12 lb) bronze turkey
groundnut oil

For the stuffing
115 g (4 oz) pine nuts
675 g (1½ lb) spinach
175 g (6 oz) dried apricots, soaked overnight and chopped

175 g (6 oz) fresh brioche crumbs
1 heaped teaspoon finely chopped fresh rosemary
1 teaspoon finely chopped fresh thyme
sea salt and black pepper

Preheat the oven to 180°C (fan oven)/190°C (375°F) gas 5 and toast the pine nuts for 5 minutes. Blanch the spinach in boiling salted water, drain thoroughly and chop. Combine all the ingredients for the stuffing, including the spinach and toasted pine nuts, in a large bowl. Cool completely. Turn the oven up to 200°C (fan oven)/220°C (425°F) gas 7.

Fill the main cavity of the turkey with the stuffing, packing it loosely; leave half the cavity empty, but plug the opening. You can also stuff the neck end, using a different stuffing or half an onion with a couple of sprigs of thyme or rosemary and a piece of lemon zest. Brush the turkey all over with groundnut oil, then rub salt and pepper into the skin.

Set the turkey breast down in a large, oiled roasting tray. Protect the wings and legs with foil to prevent them from drying out. Place the turkey in the oven and roast for 30 minutes, then turn down to 180°C (fan oven)/190°C (375°F) gas 5 and continue roasting for the times suggested below. Baste periodically with the juices in the roasting tray. About 30–45 minutes before the bird is cooked, turn it breast uppermost so it can brown. To check if the bird is cooked through, insert a skewer into the thickest part of the flesh, the thigh; the juices should run out clear. If not, give the bird another 10 minutes, then check again. Remove the turkey to a carving plate and leave it to rest for around 20 minutes while you make the gravy (see below).

Recommended roasting times
4.5 kg (10 lb), 2 hours; 6.75 kg (15 lb), 2³⁄₄ hours; 9 kg (20 lb), 3¹⁄₂ hours; 11.25 kg (25 lb), 4¹⁄₂ hours. Allow extra time if using aluminium foil.

Gravy*

Mention the word gravy in a professional kitchen and chef will approach you with a cleaver – the term *'jus de rôti'* is preferred. But the more flavour your bird has, the better your gravy will be, and you can help matters by roasting the giblets first. This is a simple thin gravy, in essence the flavour of the bird given back to it. Prepare the stock ahead of time and finish the gravy while the bird is resting.

For the stock
giblets (heart, liver, neck and gizzard), chopped
85 ml (3 fl oz) red wine

bouquet garni: 1 sprig thyme, 1 bay leaf, 2 parsley stalks
1 carrot, 1 leek and 1 small onion, trimmed and chopped

Preheat the oven to 200°C (fan oven)/220°C (425°F) gas 7 and roast the giblets with a little fat for 20 minutes until slightly coloured. Place in a saucepan, cover with plenty of water and bring to a gentle boil. Simmer for about 1 hour, skimming until all fat and froth is removed; top up with water if necessary. Add the wine, bouquet garni and chopped vegetables, cover and simmer for 1 hour. Strain the stock and reserve.

To finish
175 g (6 oz) mixture of leek, carrot and celery, chopped
85 ml (3 fl oz) red wine

Drain surface fat from the roasting tray. Cook the mixed vegetables with the juices that remain until syrupy and golden, add any wine and reduce by half. Add the stock and simmer for 15 minutes. Season. Strain the gravy into a sauceboat.

Honey-glazed Ham*

Serves 6

In Barbados pigs are of a fine quality. Traditionally the best cuts found their way on to the master's table, and the remainder of the animal was given to the slaves, hence dishes like 'souse' that call for pig's head and trotters. Providing it is a mild cure there is no need to soak your ham for 24 hours; check this with your butcher.

---

1 x 1.8 kg (4 lb) uncooked green gammon joint, boned

For the court-bouillon
4 cloves
8 peppercorns
2 bay leaves
3 sprigs fresh thyme
115 g (4 oz) carrot, peeled and chopped

1 small onion, peeled and chopped
3 sticks celery, sliced
1 leek, trimmed and sliced

For the glaze
115 g (4 oz) strong honey, e.g. heather
1 heaped teaspoon English mustard

Place the gammon joint in a saucepan, cover with cold water and bring to the boil. Discard the water and start again with fresh water to cover, this time adding the ingredients for the court-bouillon. Bring to the boil, cover and simmer for 45 minutes.

Preheat the oven to 140°C (fan oven)/150°C (300°F) gas 2. Remove the gammon to a roasting tray, and cut off and discard rind. Blend together the honey and mustard and coat all sides of the gammon. Pour a few millimetres of ham stock into the roasting tray and roast for 40 minutes; turn the oven up to 200°C (fan oven)/220°C (425°F) gas 7 and roast for a further 10 minutes. Allow to cool. Serve in thin slices.

Spaghetti alla Carbonara

Serves 4

Classic and chic, not least because of all that tossing with raw eggs. This recipe is based on Marcella Hazan's version in *The Second Classic Italian Cookbook*. I have only been able to find smoked pancetta in my nearby delis, so I use unsmoked back bacon since smoke is so overwhelming.

---

2 tablespoons extra virgin olive oil

15 g (½ oz) unsalted butter

4 cloves garlic, peeled and lightly crushed

225 g (8 oz) unsmoked back bacon, cut into strips 1 x 2.5 cm (½ x 1 inch)

4 tablespoons white wine

450 g (1 lb) spaghetti

3 eggs (size 2)

85 g (3 oz) freshly grated Parmesan

2 tablespoons finely chopped fresh flat-leaf parsley

sea salt and black pepper

Place the oil, butter and garlic in a frying pan and cook until the garlic turns golden, then remove and discard it. Add the bacon and fry until it turns crisp at the edges. Add the wine and cook for about 1 minute, then remove from the heat.

Bring a large pan of salted water to the boil and cook the spaghetti, leaving it firm to the bite. Lightly beat the eggs in a large bowl, blend in the Parmesan and the parsley and season well. Drain the spaghetti, though not too thoroughly, and rapidly toss into the egg and cheese mixture. Quickly reheat the bacon, drain off fat and toss into the pasta. Serve straightaway.

FISH

Poached Seabass with Herbs in Oil*

Serves 4

This is a special dish, very simple; boiled potatoes and a few steamed vegetables or a salad are all you need to accompany it. It is also good cold the next day.

---

1 x 1.3 kg (3 lb) seabass, or 2 smaller fish, gutted and cleaned

For the dressing
15 g (½ oz) fresh chives, snipped into 1 cm (½ inch) lengths
1 heaped tablespoon finely chopped fresh flat-leaf parsley
2 teaspoons finely chopped fresh chervil
¼ teaspoon finely chopped fresh thyme
¼ teaspoon finely chopped garlic

lemon juice
1 teaspoon balsamic vinegar
175 ml (6 fl oz) extra virgin olive oil

For the poaching liquor
1.2 litres (2 pints) water
600 ml (1 pint) white wine
1 carrot, peeled and sliced
1 onion, chopped
1 stick celery, sliced
1 bay leaf
2 parsley stalks
1 heaped teaspoon sea salt

Mix together the dressing ingredients and leave to stand for 1 hour. Place all the ingredients for the poaching liquor in a fish kettle, or other suitable pan with a lid, and bring to the boil. If not using a fish kettle with a removable grid, lower the bass into the pan using a tea towel as a sling; you will then be able to lift it out easily. If the fish is too long for the pan, remove head and tail. Bring to an ambling boil, then cover the pan and poach for 16 minutes for one large fish, slightly less for 2 smaller ones.

Lift the fish on to a serving dish and remove the skin. Serve filleted, with the dressing spooned over.

Rappie Pie with Sorrel Sauce*

Serves 4

This has nostalgic roots: summer in the Outer Hebrides. Cockles are there for the digging as long as you know your beaches and tides, and surrounding the house where we were staying, growing wild amongst the long grasses, was lots of sorrel.

Rappie pie is like a rosti flavoured with clam juices, though cockles work beautifully too. The creamy sorrel and watercress sauce is essential, but if sorrel is hard to find, flavour the sauce with chervil, chives or just plenty of watercress.

For the pie
900 g (2 lb) cockles, or use palourdes or similar clams
1.6 kg (3½ lb) maincrop potatoes
1 small onion
black pepper
25 g (1 oz) unsalted butter

For the sauce
85 g (3 oz) shallots
25 g (1 oz) unsalted butter
150 ml (¼ pint) dry vermouth
150 ml (¼ pint) white wine
450 ml (¾ pint) double-strength fish stock
450 ml (¾ pint) double cream
25 g (1 oz) sorrel, sliced
15 g (½ oz) watercress leaves
sea salt and black pepper

To make the pie, wash the cockles or clams in a sink of cold water, discarding any that are broken or do not close when sharply tapped. Steam them open over a high heat for 3–5 minutes. Shell them, and reserve meat and juice separately.

Preheat the oven to 200°C (fan oven)/220°C (425°F) gas 7. Peel and coarsely grate the potatoes: a food processor will make light work of this. Place one handful of potato at a time in a tea towel and wring out as much juice as possible into a measuring jug; reserve the squeezed-out potato in a bowl. Peel and grate the onion and combine with the potato. Check the quantity of potato juice, then discard it. Measure out an equal quantity of cockle juice – about 150 ml (¼ pint) – and mix it with the potato pulp, which will absorb it; discard the last little bit of gritty cockle juice. Season the mixture with pepper.

Choose a gratin dish at least 5 cm (2 inches) deep and grease with half the butter. Press half the potato mixture into it, scatter over the cockles and then press the remaining potato on top. Dot with the rest of the butter and bake for 55–60 minutes until golden and crisp on the surface.

To make the sauce, peel and slice the shallots. Melt the butter in a saucepan and sweat the shallots for a few minutes until soft but not coloured. Add the vermouth and wine and reduce to a syrup. Add the fish stock and cook for a few minutes, then add the cream and cook until the sauce thickens slightly. Strain the sauce and return it to the pan. Add the sorrel and watercress; as soon as the sorrel turns a dull green, liquidise the sauce and season. (The sauce can be made in advance and reheated.) Serve it poured over the pie.

Seafood Tagliatelle with Garlic and Parsley

Serves 4

Antonio Carluccio recommended this simple, quick recipe. Scallops and mussels are a good combination, but the seafood can be varied, depending on what shellfish are available. Although the scallop coral looks wonderful, it is not especially pleasant to eat, so you may prefer to discard it. The addition of chilli gives the dish a nice piquancy. For added sophistication, serve half black pasta, coloured with sepia or squid ink, and half white pasta.

---

900 g (2 lb) mussels, cleaned
12 medium-size scallops
400 g (14 oz) tagliatelle
6 tablespoons extra virgin olive oil
1 clove garlic, peeled and finely chopped

1 heaped teaspoon finely chopped fresh red chilli
sea salt and black pepper
2 tablespoons finely chopped fresh flat-leaf parsley

Steam the mussels open in a covered pan for 5 minutes. Shell them, reserving a handful shell-on as a garnish. Keep moist with a little of the liquor. Pour the remaining liquor into a clean saucepan, discarding the last little gritty bit, and reduce to a couple of tablespoons. Scrape the scallops clean if necessary (avoid washing them) and remove gristle at the side, hence separating the coral. Slice the scallops into 5 mm (1/4 inch) rounds.

Bring a large pan of salted water to the boil and put the pasta on to cook. Heat the olive oil in a large frying pan and add the garlic and chilli. When the garlic gives off an aroma, add the seafood and cook for about 1 minute, stirring. Add the reduced mussel liquor to the frying pan. Drain the pasta and mix with the seafood. Adjust seasoning and toss in the parsley. Serve garnished with unshelled mussels.

Prawns with Garlic

Serves 2–4

In Seville this is a typical *tapa*, or occasionally it would extend into lunch with a basket of bread to mop up the garlicky juices.

---

3 tablespoons extra virgin olive oil	2 tablespoons dry sherry
450 g (1 lb) uncooked Dublin Bay prawns (langoustines)	3 tablespoons white wine
	sea salt and black pepper
	20 g (³/₄ oz) unsalted butter
3 cloves garlic, peeled and finely chopped	finely chopped fresh flat-leaf parsley

---

Heat the oil in a frying pan and cook the prawns for 4–5 minutes. Shell them once cool, leaving the tail-fans attached; reserve the prawns.

Add the garlic to the pan and cook it for a minute, then add the sherry and wine and season the sauce. Reduce it by half, adding the prawns to heat through just before the end. Remove the prawns to a bowl. Whisk the butter into the reduction and coat the prawns with this. Scatter over the parsley and serve.

Smoked Salmon with a Cucumber Salad and Caviar

Serves 4–6

Fresh caviar has less salt than the pasteurised variety. Sevruga is the bottom of the range and the most assertive in flavour, Osietra is in the middle, and Beluga is what one assumes kings have for breakfast. If you want to fake it, go for salmon keta roe. The common lumpfish roe seems to contain more additives than eggs and tastes accordingly.

Most of the water is squeezed from the cucumber – lightly dressed with vinegar and sugar, it has a hint of pickle about it and acts as a foil to the richness of the salmon.

2 cucumbers	6 heaped teaspoons soured
sea salt	cream
1 tablespoon sherry vinegar	at least 25 g (1 oz) caviar
1 level teaspoon caster sugar	450 g (1 lb) smoked salmon
black pepper	1 lemon, quartered

Peel the cucumbers and slice wafer thin. Arrange in layers in a colander, sprinkling each layer with salt. Leave for 45 minutes, then rinse thoroughly. Place half the cucumber in a tea towel and squeeze out most of the moisture: be careful not to overdo this. Repeat with the other half. Place the cucumber in a bowl and mix in the vinegar, sugar and pepper.

To serve, place a pile of cucumber in the centre of each of 6 plates and put a teaspoon of soured cream and 1/2 teaspoon of caviar on top. Surround with smoked salmon. Squeeze a little lemon juice on the salmon and grind black pepper over.

Chilled Chinese Egg Noodles with Sesame and Crab

Serves 4

Icy noodles are perfect for really hot weather.

---

200 g (7 oz) mangetouts
225 g (8 oz) Chinese egg noodles
225 g (8 oz) white and brown
  crab meat, picked over
2 heaped tablespoons coarsely
  chopped fresh coriander
  leaves
2 heaped tablespoons sesame
  seeds, toasted
4 spring onions, trimmed and
  thinly sliced

For the dressing
2 tablespoons lime juice
2 tablespoons light soy sauce
1 teaspoon light sesame oil
2 tablespoons groundnut oil
5 tablespoons fish stock
$1/8$–$1/4$ teaspoon chilli powder
$1/2$ teaspoon caster sugar

Bring a large pan of salted water to the boil. Top and tail the mangetouts and cut into strips; blanch for 30 seconds. Remove with a slotted spoon, plunge into cold water and reserve. Cook the noodles in the same water for 4–5 minutes until just done. Drain in a sieve and run cold water through them. Combine the noodles and mangetouts in a bowl, cover and chill. Combine all the ingredients for the dressing. Mix 2 tablespoons of dressing with the crab.

To serve, toss the noodles with the remaining dressing and mix in the coriander and sesame seeds. Divide among 4 plates. Place the crab in a mound on top of the noodles and scatter the spring onions over.

SIDE DISHES

Spinach and Chickpeas

Serves 2–4

Espinacas con garbanzos, a common *tapa*, is deliciously rich and spiced, typically Moorish with its overtones of cumin, coriander and saffron. It plays on that successful combination of mealy pulse and succulent leaf. If you can be bothered to cook your own chickpeas this is preferable, but canned will pass.

extra virgin olive oil
550 g (1¼ lb) fresh young
   spinach leaves, washed and
   dried
2 cloves garlic, peeled and
   finely chopped
2 shallots, peeled and finely
   chopped
½ teaspoon cumin seeds,
   crushed

½ teaspoon coriander seeds,
   crushed
few strands of saffron, ground
140 g (5 oz) canned chickpeas
280 g (10 oz) tomatoes, peeled,
   deseeded and diced
sea salt and black pepper
lemon juice

Heat a tablespoon of olive oil in a frying pan and cook the spinach in batches until it wilts, adding more oil as necessary. Reserve in a bowl. Pour off any excess water before using it in the next stage.

In a medium-size saucepan cook the garlic and shallots in a little olive oil until soft. Add the spices and chickpeas and cook for 1 minute. Add the spinach, tomatoes and seasoning. Cover the pan and braise over a low heat for 10 minutes. Add an additional tablespoon of olive oil and cook uncovered for a further 10 minutes so that the remaining liquid evaporates. Adjust seasoning and sharpen with lemon juice.

Salad of Smoked Eel, Capers and Rocket

Serves 4

The pungency of the smoked eel allows you to make use of hot and spicy leaves such as rocket, and mustard and cress.

For the dressing
2 teaspoons Champagne vinegar
2 teaspoons lemon juice
sea salt
1/4 teaspoon mustard
2 tablespoons extra virgin olive oil
1 tablespoon groundnut oil

For the salad
mixture of oakleaf lettuce, radicchio or Treviso, mustard and cress, and rocket, all shredded
4 tablespoons cucumber, cut into julienne
2 teaspoons capers, finely chopped
2 spring onions, finely sliced
225 g (8 oz) smoked eel fillets

Whisk the vinegar and lemon juice with salt and the mustard, then add the oils. Place the mixed leaves in a large bowl with the cucumber, capers and spring onions. Cut the eel into 7.5 cm (3 inch) lengths. Toss the salad with the dressing, mix in the smoked eel and pile on to a large plate. Serve immediately.

Salad of Winter Chicories, Fennel and Blood Oranges

Serves 4

For the dressing
2 tablespoons red wine vinegar
sea salt and black pepper
7 tablespoons extra virgin olive oil

For the salad
2 bulbs fennel
2 heads Belgian chicory
½ head radicchio
3 blood oranges
55 g (2 oz) black olives, stoned
1 heaped tablespoon finely chopped chives

First prepare the dressing: whisk the vinegar with some seasoning, then add the oil. Remove the tough outer layers from the fennel and cut off the shoots. Slice into thin wedges, keeping them attached at the base, and steam for 2 minutes. Toss with the dressing and leave to cool.

Use the whole inner leaves of the chicory, and just the leaf section of the outer leaves. Remove tough white parts of radicchio and tear red leaf into pieces. Cut all skin and pith off the oranges and remove the segments, discarding pith that separates them. Toss all the salad ingredients together in a bowl, mixing in the fennel and dressing. Serve immediately.

Mixed Leaves with Deep-fried Herbs and Balsamic Vinaigrette

Serves 4

Deep-fried herbs are delicate and absurdly pretty. You can change the selection of salad leaves, using something slightly spicy but nothing too bitter or peppery.

For the dressing
1 teaspoon balsamic vinegar
1 teaspoon lemon juice
sea salt
1½ tablespoons extra virgin olive oil
1½ tablespoons groundnut oil

For the salad
groundnut oil for deep-frying
25 g (1 oz) mixed fresh coriander, basil and flat-leaf parsley leaves
mixture of lamb's lettuce, red Lollo, and mustard and cress

To prepare the dressing, whisk the balsamic vinegar, lemon juice and salt together, then add the oils.

Heat groundnut oil for deep-frying, but not to smoking or it will singe the leaves – they should cook instantly but retain their colour. Throw a few herb leaves at a time into the hot oil, remove with a slotted utensil and drain on kitchen paper.

Dress the salad leaves in a bowl and gently toss in the deep-fried herbs. Serve immediately.

Wild Rice Salad with Baby Corn, Coriander and Almonds*

Serves 6

This salad is an old favourite which I have served at more parties than I can remember. It is ideal for making in quantity.

For the dressing
2 teaspoons lemon juice
2 teaspoons lime juice
sea salt and black pepper
1 heaped teaspoon finely diced root ginger
1 clove garlic, peeled and crushed to a paste
2 teaspoons extra virgin olive oil
3 tablespoons groundnut oil

For the salad
85 g (3 oz) wild rice
115 g (4 oz) white rice

85 g (3 oz) fennel, cut into 5 mm (1/4 inch) dice
85 g (3 oz) sugarsnap peas, tails removed
85 g (3 oz) baby sweetcorn
extra virgin olive oil
sea salt and black pepper
3 spring onions, trimmed and finely sliced
2 heaped tablespoons flaked almonds, toasted
2 heaped tablespoons fresh coriander leaves
25 g (1 oz) radicchio, torn into pieces, white parts removed

First prepare the dressing: whisk the lemon and lime juices with salt and pepper, then add the ginger, garlic and the oils. Set aside.

Boil the wild rice in salted water for 45 minutes. Drain in a sieve and run cold water through it. Place in a bowl. Simultaneously cook the white rice in the same fashion for 15 minutes. Combine the rices.

Blanch the fennel and sugarsnap peas for 1 minute; refresh in cold water. Halve the sweetcorn lengthways, brush with olive oil, season and char-grill; or cook in a dry frying pan until patched with brown. Cool. Mix these vegetables and the spring onions with the rice. Strain the dressing.

To serve, toss the salad with the dressing, the almonds, coriander leaves and radicchio.

Saffron Potatoes

Serves 4

These are Raymond Blanc's *pommes de terre aux pistils de safran*, glazed, golden and aromatic. M. Blanc says they go well with all Provençal dishes. I have taken the liberty of replacing the chicken stock with a vegetable one.

---

15 saffron filaments, ground	2 shallots, peeled and finely
100 ml (3¹/₂ fl oz) vegetable	chopped
stock	1 sprig fresh thyme
550 g (1¹/₄ lb) new potatoes	1 bay leaf
20 g (³/₄ oz) unsalted butter	sea salt and black pepper

Cover the ground saffron with a tablespoon of boiling stock and leave for 10 minutes. Select potatoes of a similar size and peel them.

Heat the butter in a medium-sized saucepan and sweat the shallots and dried potatoes for a couple of minutes. Add the saffron, thyme, bay leaf and seasoning. Turn the potatoes until they are well coated with the saffron mixture. Add the stock and cover the potatoes with a buttered paper, then the lid. Cook for 15 minutes, stirring once. The liquid should have evaporated.

Peas and Rice*

Serves 4

'Peas' in Bajan terms means pigeon peas, which can be fresh or dried. Red kidney beans are a popular substitute, but I prefer the compact nature of aduki beans, or yellow split peas. Serve peas and rice with a soupy dish, or with a fresh tomato sauce poured over.

---

100 g (3½ oz) aduki beans or yellow split peas, soaked overnight in water and drained
2 tablespoons groundnut oil
5 spring onions, trimmed and thinly sliced
225 g (8 oz) basmati rice, soaked for 30 minutes in water and rinsed

350 ml (12 fl oz) boiling water
1 level teaspoon sea salt
2 bay leaves
1 heaped teaspoon fresh thyme leaves
3 sprigs fresh marjoram
5 cm (2 inch) stick cinnamon
1 star-anise
black pepper

Bring a pan of water to the boil and cook the beans for 35–40 minutes. Drain and rinse with boiling water.

About 10 minutes into cooking the beans, heat the groundnut oil in a saucepan and sweat the spring onions for 1–2 minutes until soft. Add the rice and cook for 1–2 minutes. Add all the remaining ingredients except for the pepper, bring to a simmer and cook for 10 minutes or until the water is absorbed. Cover tightly with a lid and allow to stand off the heat for 10 minutes.

Fluff the rice with a fork, remove the whole herbs and spices, and mix in the beans. Season with pepper.

DESSERTS

TARTS

They entice and seduce us from Lenôtre in Paris to Maison Blanc in London . . .

Tart Case*

The following two tart recipes call for tart cases using a home-made sweet shortcrust pastry, but if time is tight you can substitute a bought shortcrust.

This is Maison Blanc's recipe for *pâte sucrée*. Select a 23 cm (9 inch) tart tin with sides 2.5 cm (1 inch) deep and a removable base. Once the tart is cooked and cool you can remove the sides, and either transfer the tart to a plate or serve it straight from the base.

60 g (2¼ oz) unsalted butter, softened	½ egg (size 2)
60 g (2¼ oz) caster sugar	125 g (4½ oz) plain flour, sifted
	15 g (½ oz) ground almonds

Cream the butter and sugar together in a food processor. Mix in the egg, then add the flour and ground almonds. As soon as the dough begins to form into a ball, wrap it in clingfilm and chill for 2 hours. The dough can be kept in the fridge for several days.

Preheat the oven to 180°C (fan oven)/190°C (375°F) gas 5. Butter the tart tin. On a lightly floured surface roll out the dough 3 mm (⅛ inch) thick and line the bottom and sides of the tin, trimming the excess. Line the pastry case with baking parchment and weight with baking beans. For a part-baked case, cook for 15–20 minutes until starting to colour. Remove the paper and beans and cool before filling.

Orange Custard Tart*

Serves 6

This is a baked custard tart, an orange cream filling scented with orange flower water and with fine strips of candied orange zest streaking the surface. Glaze it with a flower jelly for additional fragrance; otherwise use an apricot jam.

---

1 part-baked tart case (see page 75)
3 eggs (size 2)
2 egg yolks (size 2)
140 g (5 oz) caster sugar
finely chopped zest of 2 oranges
125 ml (4 fl oz) orange juice
50 ml (2 fl oz) lemon juice

225 ml (8 fl oz) double cream
1 teaspoon orange flower water
1 heaped tablespoon scented jam, or sieved apricot jam

For the candied peel
1 orange
2 tablespoons caster sugar
2 tablespoons water

If any cracks have appeared in the tart case, fill these in with raw pastry dough. Preheat the oven to 130°C (fan oven)/140°C (275°F) gas 1. Whisk together the eggs and egg yolks with the caster sugar. Add the orange zest and juice, lemon juice, cream and orange flower water. Pour into the part-baked tart case and bake for 45 minutes. Remove and cool.

Peel the orange with a potato peeler, then cut the zest into fine strips. Blanch for 30 seconds in boiling water and refresh under cold running water. Heat the sugar and water together to make a syrup, add the orange zest and simmer over a low heat for 5 minutes; reserve.

Heat the sieved jam until it liquefies, and thinly glaze the surface of the tart. Decorate with a few strands of candied zest, reserving the remainder for some other use. Place in a cool place for the glaze to set.

Joel Robuchon's Plum and Almond Tart*

Serves 6

Cuisine Actuelle by Patricia Wells and Joel Robuchon is a real pleasure to cook from. This tart, based on their recipe, is rich with fruit: halved plums sit in a thin layer of almond cream that rises as it cooks. The result is very light, richly scented with the fruit. It is essential that the plums are sweet and ripe; purple plums, greengages and apricots are all suitable.

---

100 g (3½ oz) whole blanched
  almonds
70 g (2½ oz) unsalted butter,
  softened
100 g (3½ oz) caster sugar
1 egg (size 2)

1 egg white (size 2)
1 part-baked tart case (see
  page 75)
400 g (14 oz) small plums
icing sugar

Preheat the oven to 170°C (fan oven)/180°C (350°F) gas 4. Grind the almonds in an electric grinder, then combine with the butter and sugar in a food processor. Mix to a smooth cream with the egg and egg white. Smooth the almond cream on to the bottom of the pastry case. Halve the plums and place cut side up on the filling. Bake for 45 minutes until the filling is golden, risen and firm. Dust with icing sugar once cool. Serve at room temperature.

Tira-mi-su with Praline and Fresh Raspberries

Serves 4

Tira-mi-su is the ultimate coffee dessert. Espresso is too forceful, so use a strong brew of a medium-roast coffee, prepared in a cafetière: the mellow chocolate tones of Jamaica Blue Mountain cannot be bettered. An adornment of gold leaf is the most exotic decoration I have ever encountered on a tira-mi-su, but dust it with cocoa powder instead of the suggested praline if time is short. Neater than making it in a bowl is to prepare it in a square dish and serve it in slices.

---

175 ml (6 fl oz) strong black coffee, cold
85 ml (3 fl oz) Kahlua
25 g (1 oz) caster sugar
25 g (1 oz) vanilla sugar
3 eggs (size 2), separated
450 g (1 lb) mascarpone
200 g (7 oz) savoiardi or sponge fingers

framboise
350 g (12 oz) fresh raspberries
icing sugar

For the praline
25 g (1 oz) caster sugar
25 g (1 oz) flaked almonds, toasted

Combine the coffee and Kahlua in a shallow bowl. Whisk the sugars and egg yolks together and beat in the mascarpone until smooth. Whisk the egg whites until stiff and fold into the mascarpone mixture. Smear a spoon or two of the mascarpone mousse on the bottom of the chosen serving dish.

Dip sponge fingers one at a time into the coffee and Kahlua mixture until the sponge starts to yield between your fingers, but not so that it is totally sodden. Cover the bottom of the dish with a single layer of sponge fingers, and smooth some mascarpone mousse on top. Make three layers each of sponge and of mousse. Smooth the surface with a palette knife. Cover and chill for at least 2 hours, or overnight.

To prepare the praline, place the sugar in a small saucepan and cook to a golden caramel, making sure it does not burn. Mix in the almonds, then spoon into a buttered dish and leave to cool. When set, pound to a coarse powder between two tea towels using a rolling pin. Scatter a fine layer of praline over the tira-mi-su just before serving it.

Sprinkle a little framboise over the raspberries and sweeten to taste with icing sugar. Leave for 30 minutes. Serve a small pile beside the tiramisu.

Grand Pot au Chocolat

Serves 6

Petits pots au chocolat are those delectable little cups of silken chocolate cream. For a number of people it makes sense to make the cream in a single bowl and dole it out, but you can use coffee cups if you wish. I have it on the authority of some-one who eats chocolate mousse daily that this pudding is even better.

---

225 ml (8 fl oz) double cream	**85 g (3 oz) milk chocolate**
175 ml (6 fl oz) full cream milk	**140 g (5 oz) dark chocolate**
4 egg yolks, whisked	**2 teaspoons Tia Maria**

Bring the cream and milk to the boil and pour it on to the egg yolks. It should thicken to a thin custard instantly. Pass through a sieve, cover the surface with clingfilm and cool to room temperature. Melt the chocolate by chopping it into small pieces and placing it in a bowl over hot but not boiling water. Blend half the custard with the melted chocolate, and then add the rest. Stir in the Tia Maria. Spoon into a serving dish or little coffee cups, cover with clingfilm and chill.

Indian Cheesecake with Polenta Crust*

Serves 6

It is the molasses in the cream and the polenta in the crust that set this cheesecake apart, one of many tasters served on a sweet platter at Postrio in San Francisco.

For the crust
85 g (3 oz) plain flour, sifted
**40 g (1½ oz) fine-ground
  polenta**
55 g (2 oz) caster sugar
**85 g (3 oz) unsalted butter,
  melted**

For the filling
**550 g (1¼ lb) low-fat cream
  cheese**
175 g (6 oz) caster sugar
3 eggs (size 2)
150 ml (¼ pint) soured cream
**½ teaspoon pure vanilla
  essence**
pinch of salt
½ teaspoon ground ginger
½ teaspoon ground cinnamon
**2 level teaspoons molasses or
  black treacle**

Preheat the oven to 140°C (fan oven)/150°C (300°F) gas 2. Mix the ingredients for the crust together in a bowl to make a dough. Using your fingers, press this on to the bottom of a 20 cm (8 inch) cake tin with a removable collar. Bake for 35 minutes until pale gold; allow to cool.

To prepare the filling, blend together the cream cheese and sugar in a food processor or electric mixer. Add the eggs one at a time, then the soured cream and remaining ingredients, adding the molasses last. Strain the mixture into the tin on top of the crust and bake for 40 minutes. The centre of the filling should quiver when gently shaken – it will set more firmly as it cools. Run a knife around the edge of the tin to prevent the filling cracking as it cools. Once cool, cover and chill overnight or for several hours. Remove the collar and serve.

Jasmine Crème Brûlée*

Serves 4

---

200 ml (7 fl oz) boiling water	115 g (4 oz) caster sugar
1 tablespoon jasmine tea	400 ml (14 fl oz) double cream
leaves	demerara sugar
6 egg yolks (size 2)	

Preheat the oven to 140°C (fan oven)/150°C (300°F) gas 2. Pour the boiling water over the tea leaves in a jug or a pot and infuse for 5 minutes. Strain the tea and reserve. Whisk the egg yolks and caster sugar together, whisk the cream into this mixture and stir in the strained tea. Pass through a sieve into a 20 cm (8 inch) heatproof dish.

Place the dish in a bain-marie so that the boiling water is level with the surface of the custard. Cook for 1 hour or until it has set. Once it is cool, cover with clingfilm and chill for a couple of hours.

Preheat the grill. Grind some demerara sugar in an electric grinder and sieve a fine film over the surface of the custard. Place under the grill until molten and bubbling. Repeat with a second film of sugar. Return to the fridge until this is hard. Do the caramelising close to the time of serving.

Earl Grey Trifle

Serves 6

Tea jellies are the sort of old-fashioned preserve you expect to find in Fortnum and Mason, but Sainsbury's now stock an Earl Grey jelly in its special selection department. You can, of course, use another jam or jelly. If you want a lighter trifle use half mascarpone and half fromage frais.

---

2 ripe peaches or nectarines
1 level tablespoon caster sugar
2 egg yolks (size 2)
450 g (1 lb) mascarpone
3 egg whites (size 2)
55 g (2 oz) vanilla sugar, or use
   caster sugar
140 g (5 oz) sponge cake,
   sliced 5 mm (¼ inch) thick

85 ml (3 fl oz) strained Earl
   Grey tea, made to treble
   strength
115 g (4 oz) Earl Grey jelly

To serve
1 passionfruit

Skin the peaches (or nectarines) by plunging them into boiling water for 30 seconds, then into cold water before peeling. Halve, remove the stone and slice thinly. Place in a bowl and sprinkle over the caster sugar. Leave for 10 minutes, then drain thoroughly.

To prepare the mousse, beat the egg yolks and mascarpone together in a large bowl until smooth. In another bowl whisk the egg whites until they hold their shape. Gradually sprinkle over the vanilla sugar and whisk well with each addition until you have a glossy meringue. Fold this, a third at a time, into the mascarpone mixture.

Assemble the trifle in a deep 20 cm (8 inch) glass bowl. First smear a spoon of mousse over the bottom. You will need two layers of each component, arranging them as follows: a layer of sponge drizzled with tea, spread with jelly, some peach slices, followed by some more mousse. Repeat this with the remaining ingredients, ending with a layer of mousse. Cover and chill for several hours or overnight. To serve, halve the passionfruit and spoon the seeds over the surface.

OUTDOOR EATING

BARBEQUES

Faking the spirit of a barbeque is virtually impossible. This I know because I've tried. Magazines are such that your deadline for finished copy is three months before it appears on the shelf. For the cookery writer this means Christmas in August, chilled soups in January. But most bizarre of all is barbeques in February.

Nothing can be guaranteed to work unless it really has been tested. So one freezing, blue-grey February day, when the light faded at around 3 pm, my husband kindly set up the barbeque yards away from the bank of an icy Thames where swans huddled close to the reeds. It was an imposing spread of duck breasts, and scallops, squid and mackerel. We wrapped up in woolly hats, impenetrable gloves, mufflers, tights under trousers and so forth, and lit the coals.

And lo and behold, the minute the embers settled down to that quietly fierce, warm orange glow, it began to snow. Not just a light dusting either – it gathered momentum until there was a thick blizzard that coated eyelashes and gathered in drifts in the creases of clothes. Still, all in a day's work, we soldiered on and ate the proceeds indoors. But if I am brutally honest I have to admit that it didn't taste quite right.

I am pleased to say that as I write this introduction it is a sweltering 90 degrees outside, and I cannot think of a more enticing way of spending the early evening, pre-prandial underway, than wandering round the garden gathering some herbs and leaves for a green salad while my husband lights up the barbeque. I shall make no apology for the sexism here – one reason why barbeques make for relaxing entertaining is that the cooking is usually shared.

The first courses I have suggested are hot weather appeasers: a small bowl of chilled gazpacho, or a silky avocado soup with a dollop of salsa. There is also a Caribbean recipe for Callalloo, which can be eaten hot or at room temperature, a wonderful gloopy concoction with okra, coconut milk and crab. And beyond that a Caesar Salad – a personal all-time favourite.

Vegetarians deserve to be especially well looked after, because barbeques are an area where many cooks come unstuck on inspiration: I have been served one too many desiccated vegetable kebabs in my time. In fact there's nothing wrong with vegetable kebabs; I malign them unfairly. Chunks of aubergine, red pepper and courgette, interspersed with mushrooms, basted with oil as they grill, can be smoky and succulent. And a dollop of something rich and zesty will not go amiss: a pastis mayonnaise or tomato butter, perhaps, or a garlicky skordalia or romesco that will mask any accidental charring.

The most memorable barbeques I have given have been the all-singing-all-dancing affairs of friends, children, brothers, sisters and grandparents. And they are usually a feast of seafood that is fast to cook and looks spectacular, like a whole barbequed fish: one year it was a wild salmon steamed between long, wet wild grasses on the grid, a heap of samphire dripping with melted butter on the table, a jug of citrus hollandaise and some Jersey Royals to partner the fish.

Amongst other seafood ideas, you could thread small squid on to skewers, paint them with chilli oil and grill them until they puff up into cushions. Scallops can be seared in a frying pan on top of the grid or lined up in a brochette. King prawns should be cooked in their shell for the best flavour. Thick slabs of tuna can be briefly seared, or marinated and made into kebabs. You may also be partial to octopus or sardines, which are most conveniently cooked lined up in one of those clamps.

But I suspect that if you asked most people to name their favourite barbequed food they would say chicken: a sticky thigh, with blackened, crispy skin, and much licking of the fingers as you go. You have probably already mastered the art of this one, so I give you just one recipe, another Caribbean classic called Bajun seasoning – with onion, chilli, thyme and lime juice.

By the time you get around to thinking about pudding, the party may have changed mood – certainly in the evening. I am not quite sure why being out of doors should lead people to drink massively more than they usually do, but it does. Keeping warm – well that's one excuse – plus all that oxygen and the freedom of open space tend to make for wild endings. Keep grilling: whole figs; or peeled and halved apples painted with melted butter and sprinkled with vanilla sugar; or peaches, apricots and bananas. Having roasted your fruits on the grid, heat a small ladle of brandy or rum, ignite it and flambé the fruits. It does seem the most appropriate finale.

STARTERS

Avocado Soup with Tomato Salsa

Serves 4

This soup has a deliciously limpid consistency, and is really quite thick. The problem of the muddy brown that avocado soups turn is overcome by making a base with all the ingredients bar the avos, chilling this, and then reliquidising the base with the avocados immediately before eating.

For the soup
1 heaped teaspoon finely
  chopped shallot
1 heaped teaspoon finely
  chopped lemon grass
2 tablespoons lemon juice
150 ml (¼ pint) double cream
300 ml (½ pint) milk
350 ml (12 fl oz) vegetable
  stock
sea salt and black pepper
4 Hass avocados, or avocados
  of a similar size

For the salsa
280 g (10 oz) beefsteak
  tomatoes, skinned,
  deseeded and diced
2 tablespoons extra virgin
  olive oil
sea salt and black pepper
sugar
1 teaspoon light soy sauce
1 teaspoon lemon juice
1 level tablespoon chopped
  fresh coriander

Place all the ingredients for the soup – except for the avocados – in a liquidiser and blitz. Chill this until you want to eat. Combine all the ingredients for the salsa in a bowl.

To serve, halve the avocados, scoop out the flesh and liquidise with the soup base until smooth. Serve in bowls with the salsa spooned over the top.

Gazpacho with Prawns

Serves 4

On occasions I like to spend time making a really special gazpacho that will star, but one of the beauties of this soup is that
you can also make a perfectly passable version by whizzing up
a few ingredients in the blender. As for the bits that traditionally accompany it, I prefer a spoon of crab meat dressed with
olive oil, or a few freshly shelled prawns, and perhaps some
tiny croutons and a little chopped parsley.

---

900 g (2 lb) plum tomatoes
1 red pepper
1 cucumber
1/2 small onion, peeled
1 garlic clove, peeled
1 teaspoon finely chopped
    fresh red chilli
1 teaspoon red wine vinegar
5 tablespoons extra virgin olive
    oil

1/2 teaspoon sugar
sea salt and black pepper

To serve
140 g (5 oz) peeled cooked
    prawns
extra virgin olive oil
chopped fresh flat-leaf parsley

Combine the vegetables in a bowl as you prepare them: chop
the tomatoes; remove core and seeds from the pepper and
chop; peel skin from the cucumber and cut into chunks. Add the
onion, garlic and chilli.

Place the vinegar, olive oil, sugar and seasoning in the blender
and start to liquidise the vegetables; you will need to do this in
batches. Press through a sieve into a large bowl. Adjust seasoning. Now liquidise again until the soup is really smooth. Chill until
required.

Serve with a spoon of prawns in the centre of each bowl, a
generous drizzle of olive oil and a sprinkling of parsley.

Callaloo with Thyme-Lime Cream

Serves 6

This soup is one of the most famous dishes of the West Indies, traditional slave fare. Callaloo is the spinach-like leaf of the eddo or malanga, both varieties of the same plant. Recipes for the soup vary, some including pigeon peas and salt fish. This is my own interpretation. Canned coconut milk and frozen crab meat make sensible labour-saving.

For the callaloo
450 g (1 lb) young spinach
    leaves
2 tablespoons groundnut oil
1 onion, peeled and finely
    chopped
2 cloves garlic, peeled and
    finely chopped
1 teaspoon finely chopped
    fresh red chilli
115 g (4 oz) okra, trimmed and
    sliced
1 sprig fresh thyme
1/4 teaspoon ground turmeric
pinch of ground saffron
850 ml (1 1/2 pints) vegetable
    stock
sea salt and black pepper

1 x 400 ml (14 fl oz) can
    coconut milk
280 g (10 oz) white crab meat,
    picked over
dash of hot pepper sauce or
    Tabasco

For the thyme-lime cream
3 tablespoons crème fraîche
1/4 teaspoon finely grated lime
    zest
1 tablespoon lime juice
1 heaped teaspoon finely
    chopped fresh thyme
2 heaped teaspoons finely
    chopped fresh flat-leaf
    parsley
sea salt and black pepper

Wash and dry the spinach leaves and shred them 5 mm (1/4 inch) thick. Heat the oil in a large saucepan and sweat the onion and garlic over a moderate heat until translucent but not coloured. Add the chilli, okra, thyme and spices and cook for 2–3 minutes. Add the spinach in 3 batches and cook over a high heat until it wilts. Add the stock and seasoning and bring to the boil, then cover and simmer for 15 minutes. Add the coconut milk, crab meat and pepper sauce and heat to just below boiling point; adjust salt.

To prepare the thyme-lime cream, blend all the ingredients together in a bowl. Serve the soup in warm bowls with a teaspoon or two of the thyme-lime cream spooned over the top.

Caesar Salad

Serves 2–4

---

2 large slices white bread, 1 cm
  (½ inch) thick
olive oil for frying
1 cos lettuce
55 g (2 oz) freshly grated
  Parmesan

For the dressing
2 eggs (size 2)
½ clove garlic, peeled and
  chopped
2 tablespoons lemon juice
2 teaspoons Worcestershire
  sauce
150 ml (¼ pint) extra virgin
  olive oil
sea salt and black pepper

First prepare the dressing: boil the eggs for 1 minute, cool under cold water and then shell them into a liquidiser, scooping out the cooked white that clings to the shell. Add the remaining ingredients and whizz to a pale emulsion.

Cut the bread into 1 cm (½ inch) cubes. Heat enough olive oil in a frying pan for shallow-frying, add the bread cubes and cook, tossing constantly, until they are golden and crisp. Remove and cool on kitchen paper.

Remove the tough outer leaves of the lettuce, and cut off the base and very tips of the leaves. Cut the lettuce across into 1 cm (½ inch) slices, wash and dry thoroughly, and arrange in a large salad bowl. Pour over the dressing and lightly mix in the Parmesan. Scatter the croutons over the top and serve straight-away.

Pan Molle with Anchovies

Serves 4

This is a glamorised rendition of panzanella, the salad that makes such good use of yesterday's bread. Make sure the bread is coarse in texture.

For the wine solution
125 ml (4 fl oz) white wine
85 ml (3 fl oz) water
1 sprig fresh rosemary
2 bay leaves
2 cloves

For the salad
3 beefsteak tomatoes
¾ cucumber
1 small red onion, peeled
1 red or orange pepper

3 tablespoons shredded
  radicchio
3 large fresh basil leaves,
  finely sliced
2 teaspoons lemon juice
1 teaspoon sherry vinegar
extra virgin olive oil
sea salt
4 slices day-old white bread,
  1 cm (½ inch) thick
55 g (2 oz) salted anchovies,
  cut into thin strips

Combine the ingredients for the wine solution in a saucepan and bring to the boil, then pour into a shallow bowl and allow to cool. Skin the tomatoes, quarter, deseed and cut into 5 cm (2 inch) strips. Prepare the cucumber in the same way. Slice the onion into strips. Peel and core the pepper, remove ribs and seeds, and cut into 5 cm (2 inch) strips. Place these vegetables together in a bowl.

Just before serving, mix in the radicchio and basil, and toss with the lemon juice, vinegar and sufficient oil to coat everything. Season with salt. Toast the bread. Spoon some of the wine solution over both sides so the bread is moistened but not sodden, and place one slice on each plate. Pile the vegetables on the bread, scatter the anchovies over and anoint generously with olive oil.

VEGETARIAN

Smoky Aubergine Salad with Cinnamon Goat's Cheese*

Serves 4

For the aubergine salad
3 tablespoons extra virgin olive oil
1 heaped teaspoon ground cumin
1 heaped teaspoon paprika
pinch of cayenne pepper
2 cloves garlic, peeled, finely chopped and crushed to a paste with salt
450 g (1 lb) beefsteak tomatoes, peeled, deseeded and diced
3 large aubergines, 350–400 g (12–14 oz) each

sea salt
lemon juice
1 heaped tablespoon finely chopped fresh coriander

For the goat's cheese
175 g (6 oz) soft, mild goat's cheese
2 tablespoons fromage frais
1/4 teaspoon freshly ground cinnamon

Heat the olive oil in a frying pan. Add the spices and, moments later, the garlic, then the tomato. Cook for 7 minutes until you have a thick, homogenous sauce, stirring frequently.

Prick the aubergines and barbeque them until they are blackened on all sides and the skin is wrinkled, about 25–35 minutes. When cool enough to handle remove the skin (I use rubber gloves and do it while hot). Place the flesh in a sieve and press out the liquid. Chop or dice the flesh.

Combine the aubergine with the sauce. Season with plenty of salt and sharpen with lemon juice. Stir in the coriander.

Blend the goat's cheese with the fromage frais and cinnamon. Serve the aubergine salad at room temperature, accompanied by the goat's cheese.

Tofu, Tomato and Onion Kebabs with Pastis Butter

Serves 4 (8 skewers)

Tofu is excellent barbequed, picking up the smoky flavour beautifully and turning crisp at the edges. Both the kebabs and the butter can be made in advance.

For the kebabs	For the pastis butter
400 g (14 oz) tomatoes	**115 g (4 oz) unsalted butter**
280 g (10 oz) red onions	**2 heaped tablespoons chopped**
450 g (1 lb) tofu, cut into 2.5 cm	**fresh dill**
(1 inch) cubes	**2 teaspoons lemon juice**
extra virgin olive oil	**1 tablespoon Pernod or other**
sea salt and black pepper	**pastis**

To make the kebabs, remove a cone at the top of each tomato to take out the core, and quarter them. Peel the onions and cut into wedges. Thread the tofu, tomato and onion alternately on to 23-cm (9-inch) skewers. Place in a shallow dish, pour over plenty of olive oil and season; turn them over and repeat. Barbeque the kebabs until nicely browned around the edges.

To make the pastis butter, cream all the ingredients together with seasoning in a food processor. Remove to a bowl, cover and chill until required.

As soon as the kebabs are cooked dot them with plenty of pastis butter and allow it to melt.

Barbequed Corn-on-the-Cob with Marjoram and Garlic*

Serves 4

It took an American relative to teach me the ins and outs of barbequing corn. Sunny yellow cobs smouldering away on the grid may look appetising but this produces an inedibly tough offering. The secret is to steam-barbeque them within the husk, and then they are heaven.

---

4 cobs sweetcorn, with husks
115 g (4 oz) unsalted butter
2 heaped teaspoons finely
    chopped fresh marjoram

2 cloves garlic, peeled, finely
    chopped and crushed to a
    paste with salt
2 teaspoons light soy sauce
black pepper

Peel back the husks, doing this carefully so they remain attached, and pull out the fine, hair-like silk. Return the husks to cover the cob and tie them in place with string. Soak in cold water for 30 minutes, then squeeze out excess water and barbeque for 15–25 minutes.

While the sweetcorn is cooking heat the remaining ingredients together in a small saucepan. Serve the butter warm, poured over the husked corn-on-the-cob.

FISH

Barbeque techniques and timings for fish differ so greatly, depending on the set-up, that there is little point in instructing you. The following are recipes for sauces and ideas of what they should accompany, but all the sauces are fairly accommodating, so do think beyond what I have suggested.

Seared Squid with Red Pepper Salsa

Serves 4

This is a raw salsa, like a little salad, and goes exceptionally well with briefly cooked squid. Cut the tomatoes and pepper into neat, even-shaped dice, and serve the salsa freshly made.

---

2 beefsteak tomatoes, skinned, deseeded and diced
2 red peppers, peeled, deseeded and diced
juice of 1 lime
2 tablespoons extra virgin olive oil

½ red onion, finely chopped
1 level teaspoon finely chopped fresh red chilli
2 heaped teaspoons chopped fresh coriander
sea salt

Combine ingredients in a bowl. Leave to stand for 30 minutes before serving.

Barbequed Grey Mullet with Bruno's Piccalilli

Serves 4

This is Bruno Loubet's celebrated piccalilli. Partner it with a characterful fish such as grey mullet.

---

2 tablespoons olive oil
1 red pepper, deseeded and finely diced
115 g (4 oz) carrots, peeled and finely diced
2 shallots, peeled and finely diced
1/2 cauliflower, cut into tiny florets
1 tablespoon white wine vinegar
250 ml (9 fl oz) white wine
50 ml (2 fl oz) water

1 level teaspoon ground ginger
1/2 teaspoon turmeric
1/2 teaspoon mild curry powder
1 heaped teaspoon sugar
1 bay leaf
sea salt
1 teaspoon cornflour blended with 1 tablespoon water
115 g (4 oz) courgettes, finely diced
1 teaspoon Meaux mustard
2 teaspoons chopped fresh coriander

Heat the olive oil in a saucepan and sweat the pepper, carrots, shallots and cauliflower for a few minutes. Add the vinegar, wine, water, spices, sugar, bay leaf and salt and simmer for 17 minutes. Stir in the cornflour mixture and the courgettes and cook for a couple of minutes longer until it thickens. Remove to a bowl to cool, then remove the bay leaf and stir in the mustard and coriander.

King Prawns with a Spiced Papaya Sauce

Serves 4

This spiced papaya sauce is sweet and intense, a recipe given to me by Leslie Alexander, the chef at Cobblers' Cove in Barbados. Thread raw unshelled prawns on to skewers, brush with olive oil and season, then char-grill.

900 g (2 lb) ripe papayas	**25 g (1 oz) caster sugar**
1 level teaspoon mild curry	**sea salt**
powder	**lime juice**

Cut the skin off the papayas, halve and scrape out the seeds. Cut the flesh into pieces, place in a liquidiser and reduce to a purée; you should have about 400 ml (14 fl oz). Singe the curry powder in a saucepan. As soon as it releases its aroma add the papaya purée; stand well back as it will splutter fiercely. Add the sugar. When the mixture comes to a simmer, cover and cook for 20 minutes, stirring occasionally. Remove to a bowl and cool, then season with salt and a generous squeeze of lime juice. Serve at room temperature with the king prawns. It will keep, covered, in the fridge for several days.

Seared Tuna with Lentils in Soy-Wasabi Butter

Serves 4

'How would you like your tuna?' has replaced 'How would you like your steak?' in California. Serve this on a bed of puréed sweet, or ordinary, potatoes and some cooked spinach – both can be made in advance.

---

900 g (2 lb) fresh tuna steak, about 2.5 cm (1 inch) thick, skin and bone removed
olive oil
sea salt and black pepper

For the lentils
115 g (4 oz) Puy lentils
150 ml (¼ pint) white wine
1 tablespoon white wine or Champagne vinegar

55 g (2 oz) shallots, peeled and finely chopped
1 heaped teaspoon wasabi
1 scant tablespoon dark soy sauce
200 g (7 oz) unsalted butter, cubed
3 tablespoons fresh coriander leaves

Bring a pan of water to the boil and cook the lentils for 25 minutes; drain. Meanwhile, prepare the butter sauce: place the wine, vinegar and shallots in a small pan, bring to a simmer and cook until only 1–2 tablespoons of liquor remain. Strain the reduction and return to the pan. Add the wasabi and soy sauce. Whisk in the butter, working on and off the heat, but don't boil. Add the warm lentils and coriander leaves and adjust seasoning. You can keep this warm over a very low heat while you barbeque the tuna.

Paint the tuna with olive oil and season it, then barbeque over hot coals so it remains medium-rare, nicely pink in the centre. Serve the tuna on top of the lentils.

Barbequed Fennel and Oyster Mushrooms with Lemon-Anchovy Mayonnaise

Serves 4 (8 skewers)

For the mayonnaise
350 ml (12 fl oz) groundnut oil
3 anchovy fillets, coarsely
   chopped
finely grated zest of 1 large
   lemon
2 egg yolks (size 2)
1 scant tablespoon lemon
   juice

For the kebabs
4 small bulbs fennel
350 g (12 oz) oyster
   mushrooms
extra virgin olive oil
sea salt and black pepper

To serve
watercress sprigs

Liquidise 50–85 ml (2–3 fl oz) of the oil with the anchovy fillets and lemon zest. Make a mayonnaise by placing the egg yolks in a bowl and gradually whisking in the remaining oil, adding the anchovy oil last. As the mayonnaise becomes too thick to whisk, add half the lemon juice, then continue adding the oil. When all the oil is incorporated add the remaining lemon juice. Cover and keep chilled until required.

Remove the tough outer sheaf and green shoots from each fennel bulb and slice into six segments; trim mushroom stalks. Thread on to 23 cm (9 inch) skewers, alternating the vegetables. Paint with olive oil and season, then barbeque. Serve with a few watercress sprigs and a large dollop of mayonnaise.

MEAT

Duck Breasts with Sweet Tomato and Sesame Chutney*

Serves 4

Sweet and aromatic, this chutney is a beautiful, clear crimson, studded with sesame seeds and raisins. Accompany with poppadoms and thin strips of spring onion. Cook the duck breasts fat side down for most of the cooking time – the fat will protect the flesh from drying out and burns off while it is cooking.

---

4 duck breasts
sea salt and black pepper

For the chutney
225 ml (8 fl oz) Champagne or
    white wine vinegar
175 g (6 oz) caster sugar
450 g (1 lb) beefsteak tomatoes,
    skinned and chopped
1/8 teaspoon fennel seeds,
    ground

pinch each of ground mace,
    garam masala, cayenne
    pepper and ground ginger
4 cardamom pods, cracked
1 bay leaf
3/4 teaspoon sea salt
15 g (1/2 oz) raisins
2 heaped teaspoons sesame
    seeds

Heat the vinegar with the sugar until it dissolves, then add the tomatoes, all the spices, the bay leaf and salt. Cook at a steady boil for 25 minutes, then remove bay leaf and cardamom pods. Add the raisins and sesame seeds and cook over a low heat for another 8 minutes, stirring regularly. The chutney will set to a jam-like consistency on cooling.

Barbeque the duck breasts and serve with the chutney.

Chicken grilled with Bajun Seasoning

Serves 6

You cannot spend any length of time in Barbados without experiencing Bajun seasoning, a quintessentially Barbadian blend of herbs and chillies. Spread it on chicken, swordfish or tuna to be grilled. It also lends itself to vegetables.

6 boned and skinned chicken breasts

For the Bajun seasoning
25 g (1 oz) spring onions, trimmed weight
25 g (1 oz) red onion, trimmed weight
1 level teaspoon finely chopped fresh red chilli

15 g (½ oz) fresh flat-leaf parsley
1 tablespoon fresh thyme leaves
sea salt and black pepper
juice of ½ lime
3 tablespoons extra virgin olive oil

To make the seasoning mixture, finely chop together the spring onions, red onion, chilli and herbs. Mix in a bowl with salt and pepper, the lime juice and olive oil.

Score the chicken breasts 5 mm (¼ inch) deep on both sides, making the cuts about 2.5 cm (1 inch) apart. Season with salt and spread 1 heaped teaspoon of Bajun seasoning on each side, filling the cuts. Place on a plate, cover with clingfilm and chill for up to 2 hours. Barbeque the chicken over medium-hot coals, taking care not to scorch the herbs.

Spatchcocked Quail with Five-Spice*

Serves 4

This is the ultimate finger-lickin' experience – knives and forks are out of the question when it comes to quail. These cook in such a short time; they are very succulent and achieve that Eastern blend of spicy, salty, sweet and sharp.

4–6 quail

For the marinade
2 tablespoons vegetable oil
2 level teaspoons five-spice
   powder

2 tablespoons lime juice
4 level teaspoons sugar
2 tablespoons dark soy sauce
1 heaped teaspoon Dijon
   mustard

Spatchcock the quail by cutting them open from the centre of the base to the top of the breastbone and opening them out, so that the two halves remain attached. Combine all the ingredients for the marinade and steep the quail in it, ideally overnight, until they are ready to be barbequed. They will take 15–25 minutes to cook; baste them with marinade while they are cooking.

Barbequed Figs with Parma Ham and Rocket

Serves 4

Slices of ham are wrapped around warm, grilled figs, present-ed on a bed of rocket. Serve this as part of a general assembly, or alternatively as a starter.

---

8 figs
extra virgin olive oil
sea salt and black pepper
115 g (4 oz) or 8 slices Parma
    ham

a couple of handfuls of rocket
    leaves

Remove the top of each fig, brush with olive oil and season. Barbeque on all sides until cooked and nicely coloured. Cool for a few minutes, then wrap each fig in Parma ham and set on a bed of rocket leaves. Pour more olive oil over the assembly and serve.

SIDE DISHES

Green Salad with Roger Vergé's Raspberry Dressing

Serves 4–6

Use any selection of salad leaves for this, and include some fresh herbs such as chives, sprigs of chervil and parsley, and coriander leaves, plus some nasturtium or borage flowers.

The dressing has a hint of raspberries and honey, and is not too sharp. Other berries can also be used.

½ teaspoon each of coriander and fennel seeds
3 tablespoons white wine vinegar
25 g (1 oz) raspberries, chopped

sea salt and black pepper
1 level teaspoon honey
6 tablespoons extra virgin olive oil

Toast the spices in a small saucepan until aromatic. Add the vinegar and simmer to reduce by half, then add the raspberries and return to the boil, crushing the fruit to a pulp. Allow to cool, then sieve. Whisk in seasoning, honey and oil.

Tabbouleh with Green Mango*

Serves 4

Mango when unripe is still sweet, juicy and fragrant, but it is harder, and very good salad material. This is such a fresh, lively salad that it belongs in the big outdoors, and the mango somehow makes it more of a summer affair.

---

85 g (3 oz) bulgar wheat
55 g (2 oz) fresh flat-leaf
   parsley leaves
25 g (1 oz) fresh mint leaves
6 spring onions
1 small green mango
40 ml (1½ fl oz) lemon juice

½ teaspoon ground
   cinnamon
sea salt and black pepper
140 ml (4½ fl oz) extra virgin
   olive oil
2 tablespoons water

Cover the bulgar wheat with plenty of boiling water and leave it to soak for 30 minutes. Drain and place it in a bowl. Wash the herbs and coarsely chop them. Trim and finely slice the spring onions. Cut the skin off the mango, slice the flesh off the stone and cut into thin strips. Mix these ingredients with the bulgar wheat. Whisk the lemon juice with the cinnamon and seasoning, add the olive oil and 2 tablespoons of water, and use to dress the salad.

Squash Fritters

Serves 4 (Makes about 20)

These fritters disappear with alarming speed. They occupy a curious twilight zone between sweet and savoury: serve them in lieu of potatoes.

---

500 g (1 lb 2 oz) acorn or
    butternut squash (weight
    excluding skin and seeds)
55 g (2 oz) unsalted butter
25 g (1 oz) brown sugar
pinch of freshly grated nutmeg
1/2 teaspoon ground
    cinnamon

1/2 teaspoon sea salt
black pepper
85 g (3 oz) plain flour
1 teaspoon baking powder
groundnut oil for deep-frying

Coarsely chop the squash. Melt the butter in a medium-size heavy-bottomed saucepan and sweat the squash for 8 minutes over a low heat; cover and cook for another 8 minutes, stirring occasionally. Mash to a purée with the sugar, spices, salt and a grinding of pepper. Sift the flour and baking powder together and work into the purée.

Heat groundnut oil to 180°C (350°F) in a wok or other suitable pan for deep-frying – test the temperature with a thermometer. Drop heaped teaspoons of the squash mixture into the hot oil and cook for about 3–4 minutes until they are uniformly deep golden, turning them. Drain on kitchen paper and serve. You can keep them warm in a low oven for 30 minutes.

PICNICS

It is Rat in The Wind in the Willows who sums up that essential picnic feeling: 'Look here! If you've really nothing else on hand this morning, supposing we drop down the river together, and have a long day of it?' – one of the finest sentiments in the world.

And water, there's the essence of it, be it a waterfall that you can climb up to and in which you can dangle the wine on a string for chilling, or a sheltered nest you have erected in the sand dunes behind the sea, or the calm of a lakeside. I must, of course, also mention the middle of a woodland, which is the other great picnic domain.

Picnics divide broadly into spur-of-the-moment and special or smart. The former need to be organised with a certain military flourish: if one person goes and buys some fresh bread, and visits a delicatessen to buy a selection of salamis, cooked and air-cured hams, some pâté and farmhouse cheeses, then another person can rustle up the remainder of the picnic from their larder.

Useful storecupboard items to fall back on are superior cans of tuna and sardines – Ortiz and Connetable are names to look out for – as well as anchovies, sun-dried tomatoes, olives and gherkins. You may want a pot of tapenade or Gentleman's Relish, and chutney is essential: green tomato, peach, orange and date, or spiced apple. At least one fresh salad is necessary, the simplest being sliced sweet, juicy tomatoes, sprinkled with salt, caster sugar and pepper; by the time you have transported them the juices from the tomatoes will have run into a delicious liquor. You could also take olive oil along to add to this dressing.

For dessert, take your pick of summer fruits, and maybe some cantuccini for dipping in sweet wine, or spiced fruits in syrup that can be eaten with a spoon from the jar, as well as shortbread or a box of gingered Duchy Original biscuits. Chocolate is 'de rigueur', and don't worry about its pedigree – a large bar of Fruit and Nut will do nicely, a couple of rows per head to eat while lying back and contemplating.

The second type of picnic is more tricky – the smart picnic. Like Glyndebourne, Henley and Ascot. The tendency to grand menus and elaborate dishes for these occasions is frightfully British, but not terribly in the spirit of 90s entertaining. All those flavoured mousses, complex terrines and this and that en gelée are rather out of date. But special occasions do demand special food, and the recipes here are aimed at that.

Some chicken breasts that have been quietly at work in a tikka marinade, grilled shortly before you depart and served with a home-made tzatziki; a salad of char-grilled fresh tuna, new potatoes and rocket dressed with lemon juice and olive oil; or a wild rice salad studded with different vegetables and flavoured with coriander, garlic and ginger, served with langoustines. These will be memorable. Even something as straightforward as a cold roast, such as the new-season's lamb (ask your butcher to bone it so all you have to do is to roast and slice it).

Almost anything Italian is a sure-fire hit; the winning formula of olive oil, garlic and lots of herbs translates beautifully when cold. And the new Middle Eastern mood offers up all those little dishes that go to make up mezze, not only home-made hummus and taramasalata, but pastries filled with spinach, raisins and walnuts, spiked with lemon juice and allspice, plus smoky purées and Imam Bayildi, 'the swooning Imam'.

And if it really is far too hot, and life far too short, then my option would be take-away sushi, along with its wasabi, pickled ginger and soy sauce, all washed down with small glasses of iced sake, and followed up with some of those sticky Middle Eastern pastries that ooze syrup and nuts, a few punnets of wild strawberries, and a flask of jasmine tea.

Chicken Tikka

Serves 4

You can marinate the chicken tikka for up to 2 days, but give it a few hours at least. If you want finger food then cut each chicken breast into two long strips before marinating them. I gleaned this recipe from the kitchen of Gidleigh Park in Devon. For a picnic serve this at room temperature accompanied by tzatziki; it is also delicious hot. Avoid chilling the chicken once you have grilled it.

3 tablespoons extra virgin olive oil

1 garlic clove, peeled and finely chopped

1 shallot, peeled and finely chopped

5 cm (2 inch) piece of root ginger, finely chopped

1½ teaspoons five-spice powder

2 teaspoons mild curry paste

2 teaspoons white wine vinegar

grated zest and juice of 1½ limes

2 tablespoons finely chopped fresh coriander

sea salt

4 chicken breasts, skinned

Heat the olive oil in a small frying pan, about 20 cm (8 inch) in diameter, and sweat the garlic, shallot and ginger for a minute or two until soft. Add the spice powder, then the curry paste, and cook for a minute. Add the vinegar and the lime zest and juice. Remove from the heat, add the coriander, season with salt and allow to cool.

Arrange the chicken breasts and marinade in a container, cover and chill.

When ready to cook the chicken, heat a griddle or preheat the grill. Scrape most of the marinade off the chicken and grill on both sides until cooked.

Salmon Teriyaki

Serves 4

I love the Japanese understatement of this dish; refrain from Westernising it with accompanying vegetables. The skin of the salmon is beautifully crisp, and the top is glazed and lightly cooked.

If you have excess glaze it will keep in the fridge. The sake, mirin and pickled ginger are commonplace Japanese ingredients which should be found in oriental supermarkets. Mirin is a sweet cooking wine, not unlike sweet sherry but more viscous. For starter-size portions serve 115 g (4 oz) fillets; for main-course size use 175–225 g (6–8 oz) fillets.

---

15 g (½ oz) unsalted butter
1 tablespoon olive oil
4 salmon fillets, with skin

For the glaze
2 tablespoons sake
2 tablespoons mirin

4 tablespoons light soy sauce
1 tablespoon sugar

To serve
4 teaspoons pickled ginger
1 lemon

Combine the ingredients for the glaze in a saucepan and reduce until visibly thicker, about 4 minutes. Chill for several hours; it should become thick and syrupy.

Preheat the grill. Heat the butter and oil in a frying pan. When medium hot and lightly brown, add the salmon, skin side down, and cook for 6 minutes. Turn and cook the flesh side for 30 seconds. Drain on kitchen paper. Paint the flesh side generously with the glaze and grill, glazed side up, for 2 minutes. Brush the salmon with the glaze again, then leave to cool to room temperature. Serve with pickled ginger and a squeeze of lemon juice.

Middle Eastern Club Sandwich

Serves 4–6

This is a towering treasure box of Middle Eastern ingredients, layered between two halves of ciabatta. Shop-bought hummus is adequate here. Serve this in thick slices on plates with napkins.

1 beefsteak tomato, about 225 g (8 oz)	cucumber, peeled and thinly sliced
sea salt and black pepper	5 radishes, trimmed and thinly sliced
caster sugar	1 tablespoon fresh dill fronds
1 ciabatta loaf	2 tablespoons fresh coriander leaves
extra virgin olive oil	70 g (2½ oz) black olives, stoned and halved
3 spring onions, trimmed and thinly sliced	200 g (7 oz) hummus
200 g (7 oz) feta cheese, sliced	
6 cm (2½ inch) piece of	

Thinly slice the tomato, cutting across the fruit, and discard the end slices. Place the slices on a plate and season with salt, pepper and sugar. Leave for 15 minutes while you gather together the other ingredients.

To assemble: slit the ciabatta in half horizontally and pour 2 tablespoons of olive oil over each cut surface. Start building on the lower half as follows, allowing the occasional grind of black pepper (no extra salt is needed): first the tomatoes with their juices, then the spring onions and feta plus a little olive oil. Next the cucumber slices, the radishes and herbs. Scatter the olives over the cut surface of the top half and spread with hummus. Press the two halves together gently.

Salad of Asparagus and Peas with Tomato and Basil

Serves 4

When it comes to peas, fast means frozen or ready shelled, such as Marks and Spencer sells. Obviously, if you do have the time, freshly shelled are a bonus.

---

350 g (12 oz) finger-thick asparagus tips (trimmed weight)	5 tablespoons extra virgin olive oil
140 g (5 oz) shelled peas	1 beefsteak tomato, peeled, deseeded and diced
sea salt and black pepper	1 heaped tablespoon fresh basil, in fine strips
2 tablespoons white wine	
1 tablespoon lemon juice	25 g (1 oz) pine nuts, toasted

Bring a large pan of salted water to the boil and a smaller one for the peas. Peel the asparagus to within 4 cm (1½ inches) of the bottom of the tip and boil for approximately 5 minutes until just cooked. Boil fresh peas for approximately 5 minutes until cooked; boil frozen according to packet instructions. Drain the vegetables in a sieve, refresh under the cold tap and shake off water thoroughly. Season with salt and pepper and place in a bowl.

Toss with the remaining ingredients, except the pine nuts, which should be added at the last minute.

Potato Salad with Char-grilled Tuna and Rocket

Serves 4

Avoid chilling this dish. If you need to make it a day in advance, prepare and chill the potato salad, and grill the tuna before you leave.

---

550 g (1¼ lb) new potatoes
2 tablespoons white wine
2 tablespoons lemon juice
sea salt and black pepper
6 tablespoons extra virgin
   olive oil, plus extra for
   char-grilling

1 heaped tablespoon finely
   chopped red onion
900 g (2 lb) fresh tuna steaks,
   2 cm (¾ inch) thick
40 g (1½ oz) rocket

Bring a large pan of salted water to the boil and cook the potatoes for 12–15 minutes until done. Drain. If large halve or quarter them. Toss the potatoes with the wine, lemon juice, seasoning and oil, and mix in the onion. Heat a griddle or cast-iron ridged grill pan so it is very hot. Remove the skin, central bone and any dark meat from the tuna. Cut into pieces about 7.5 x 7.5 cm (3 x 3 inches), brush both sides with olive oil and season. Grill for 1½ minutes on each side – this will leave the tuna slightly pink in the centre. Arrange tuna and potato salad in a single layer in a large shallow bowl or dish, or use two. Transport the salad with the rocket on top, and toss it in at the last minute.

MORE TASTE THAN TIME

Tzatziki

Serves 4–6

Home-made tzatziki has little in common with the supermarket dips. It goes beautifully with chicken tikka, cold poached salmon and langoustines, or as part of a general mélange of dishes. This recipe comes from Rena Salaman's excellent *Greek Food*.

---

1 tablespoon extra virgin olive
  oil
1 teaspoon white wine vinegar
1 small clove garlic, peeled and
  crushed to a paste with salt
225 g (8 oz) Greek yoghurt
18 cm (7 inch) piece of
  cucumber

½ teaspoon finely chopped
  fresh mint
sea salt and black pepper

To serve (optional)
extra virgin olive oil
stoned black olives

Whisk together the olive oil, vinegar and garlic in a bowl; mix in the yoghurt. Peel the cucumber and quarter lengthwise; remove the seeds and finely dice the flesh by first slicing the quarters into thin strips. Add the cucumber and mint to the yoghurt mixture, and season. Cover and chill until required. You can serve it with a little olive oil poured over and a few black olives to garnish if you wish.

114

EVENING ENTERTAINING

The very notion of producing three courses of smart food in under 60 minutes is alarming. It goes against the grain of nature. In fact, I would go further than that and say it is virtually impossible. But I also recognise the reality that at times this is a necessity.

Rather than dividing the precious hour three ways into 20-minute slots, my own solution is to have one course that involves virtually no cooking or preparation. And I can think of a handful of cheats which involve nothing at all.

So when devising your dinner party menu, keep in mind a first course of thinly sliced, smoked wild salmon, with a grinding of black pepper and a squeeze of lemon, and a plate of buttered brown bread. Prosciutto, or air-dried ham, is in the same mould. Jazz it up with some fig quarters and a few rocket leaves.

A plate of shucked oysters is one you have probably already thought of. I cannot see the point of even the basic elaboration of shallot vinegar – I take mine virgin on bread, with a glass of chilled Sancerre.

The summer months have the advantage of all the different melons, delectably sweet and fragrant: fill half a Cantaloupe with a slug of dessert wine (infinitely preferable to port). Steamed asparagus with melted butter or hollandaise is always welcome. You may or may not be familiar with bottarga, the dried and salted roe of tuna or grey mullet: incredibly pungent and salty, grate it over spaghettini dressed with olive oil.

You can, of course, always skip the first course and instead amass a plate of hors d'oeuvres or appetisers. I love that leisurely introduction to dinner: sipping, chatting and grazing on salted almonds and olives, caper berries – the fruit of the caper bush shaped like a rugby ball – and cubes of feta that have been steeped in olive oil with chilli and herbs. More substantially, it can be a plate of salamis with roasted heads of garlic to squeeze from their casing on to bread, fresh goat's cheese, boiled quail's eggs, radishes and butter, and gherkins. One of my favourite last resorts is pitta bread, warmed in the oven and slit open, drizzled with olive oil, and sprinkled lightly with dried oregano and sea salt, or with zaatar, the Middle Eastern blend of dried thyme, sesame seeds, sumac and salt. All of these are in the spirit of tapas, which in Seville might be no more than a few slices of Manchego cheese.

It is harder to cheat at the main course. No one is going to bark at a nicely grilled Dover sole, but even then you have the vegetables to think about. It is here that one should invest the time: I find steamed veg and boiled potatoes can be boring.

Dessert is the other course where you can take the easy way out, especially during the summer months. First there are the berries: supermarkets seem to be picking up on the notion of variety, and a modern choice affords a spectacular selection of raspberries and strawberries, tayberries, loganberries and blueberries, plus, if you're lucky, some wild strawberries. Drape a few sprays of red or white currants around the edge of the bowl, dust the whole thing with icing sugar and provide a generous bowl of crème fraîche or mascarpone.

And in the winter months there are lychees and passionfruit to turn to; nuts to crack and eat with creamy Stilton; and plump dates. A ripe pear and a slice of pecorino cheese might be considered too simple for most restaurants – enjoy it at home. Or, for that matter, a chunk of farmhouse Cheddar and a Cox's apple . . .

Next step up from 'no cook' desserts come mousses, which can be whisked up in 5 minutes. Here delicate, shop-bought biscuits or chocolate thins can make a tremendous difference.

One final recommendation on the dessert front is an ice-cream maker. The most convenient are the deluxe models with their own integrated freezer that do not require pre-freezing the bowl. There is nothing wrong with the other models, but if all you have to do is flick a switch and pour in your mix then it is a different ball-game. Most ice-cream recipes recommend a custard base, but I prefer an uncooked base and use the recipe in Ben and Jerry's cookbook. They are, in my eyes, ice-cream masters. Eggs, milk, cream, sugar and flavouring – whisk and churn. Eat it freshly made while it has that seductive Mr Whippy consistency.

I forgot to mention bread. A large basket of it.

FIRST COURSES

Tom Yum Soup with Oyster Mushrooms

Serves 4–6

This soup, hot and sour with lemon grass, chillies and lime juice, is likely to shock any dormant palate into life. The recipe is based on a soup at the Thai Kitchen, 108 Chepstow Road, London W2.

450 g (1 lb) raw Dublin Bay prawns or langoustines	juice of 1 lime
1½ tablespoons groundnut oil	3 tablespoons Thai fish sauce
1.2 litres (2 pints) water	115 g (4 oz) oyster mushrooms
2 sticks lemon grass, sliced on the bias	1 tablespoon coarsely chopped fresh coriander
3 fresh lime leaves, torn	2 spring onions, trimmed and finely sliced
3 heaped teaspoons Tom Yum paste	1 teaspoon finely chopped fresh red chilli

Peel the prawns, and reserve shells and flesh separately. Heat ½ tablespoon of oil in a saucepan and cook the shells for 2 minutes. Add the water, lemon grass and lime leaves, bring to the boil and simmer, covered, for 20 minutes. Strain, discarding the solids, and return to the pan. Blend together the Tom Yum paste, lime juice and fish sauce, add to the strained liquid and cook for a further 3 minutes.

Heat the remaining oil in a frying pan and cook the mushrooms for 2 minutes until soft. Add the prawn flesh and mushrooms to the soup and cook for a couple of minutes until the prawns are opaque and firm. Serve with coriander, spring onions and chilli scattered over.

Cullen Skink

Serves 4–6

Native to the British Isles, cullen skink is a humble and reas-
suring soup that relies on good smoked haddock. Genuine
Finnan haddies are tawny in colour and, slit open, they are
long and triangular. I buy mine from a local fishmonger, who
is discerning enough to stock the real thing.

---

2 Finnan smoked haddock,
    400–425 g (14–15 oz) each
700 ml (1¼ pints) fish stock
35 g (1¼ oz) unsalted butter
sea salt and black pepper
8 shallots, peeled and finely
    chopped
175 ml (6 fl oz) Noilly Prat
⅛ teaspoon turmeric
225 ml (8 fl oz) double cream

450 g (1 lb) potatoes
1 heaped teaspoon beurre
    manié (equal quantities of
    unsalted butter and plain
    flour mashed together)
225 g (8 oz) young spinach
    leaves, blanched in boiling
    salted water
finely chopped fresh flat-leaf
    parsley to garnish

Place the fish in a pan with a few millimetres of fish stock, dot
with 10 g (¼ oz) butter and season with black pepper. Cover
with a tightly fitting lid and poach for 4–5 minutes until just cooked.
Remove bones and skin, and coarsely flake the fish; cover and
reserve. Add the cooking juices to the remaining fish stock.

Melt the remaining butter in a saucepan and sweat the shallots
until they are soft but not colouring. Add the Noilly Prat and
reduce until syrupy. Add the fish stock and turmeric and cook for
a few minutes, then add the cream and cook for another minute
or two. Strain the soup and return it to the pan (the recipe can be
prepared to this point in advance).

Peel and finely slice the potatoes, add to the hot soup and simmer, covered, for 6 minutes or until just cooked. Add the beurre
manié to thicken. Coarsely chop the spinach and add to the soup
with the haddock. Heat gently for 5 minutes. Adjust seasoning
and serve sprinkled with parsley.

Crab Mayonnaise

Serves 4

Sweet white crab meat dressed with a home-made mayonnaise, served with a few sprigs of watercress and buttered brown bread, is very hard to beat. You may prefer to leave out the garlic in the mayonnaise; I add it depending on what I feel like.

---

350 g (12 oz) white crab meat

For the mayonnaise
85 ml (3 fl oz) groundnut oil
85 ml (3 fl oz) extra virgin olive
   oil
1 clove garlic, peeled and finely
   chopped

sea salt
1 egg yolk (size 2)
½ teaspoon Dijon mustard
lemon juice

To serve
watercress sprigs

Pick over the crab meat to remove any bits of shell (do this very carefully).

Combine the oils in a jug. Sprinkle the garlic with salt and crush to a paste. Place this in a bowl with the egg yolk and the mustard and gradually start whisking in the oils. Do this in minute quantities until you are confident that the mayonnaise is thickening, then you can add the oils in larger amounts. It should be a thick glob by the end. Add a squeeze of lemon juice.

Stir the crab meat into the mayonnaise. Serve a large dollop on each plate surrounded by watercress.

Soft Herring Roes on Brioche

Serves 6

I was positively ecstatic when I first discovered herring roes, on toast, in a pub in Devon. But I would not choose to serve them if guests were in any way squeamish – it is the offal of the piscine world.

---

55 g (2 oz) unsalted butter plus
    extra for the brioche
55 g (2 oz) plain flour
1/4 teaspoon turmeric
1/2 teaspoon sea salt
675 g (1 1/2 lb) herring roes
6 slices of brioche

To serve
finely chopped fresh flat-leaf
    parsley
lemon wedges

Melt the 55 g (2 oz) of butter; skim off the surface foam, decant the crystal liquid (clarified butter) and discard the milky residue at the bottom. Blend the flour, turmeric and salt. You will need to fry the roes in 3 batches: heat some clarified butter in a frying pan, dust the roes in the seasoned flour and cook until nicely golden on both sides.

While cooking the roes, toast the brioche and butter it. Place fried roes on top, sprinkle with parsley and serve lemon wedges separately.

Carpaccio of Salmon with Dill

Serves 6

The salmon is thinly sliced, then brushed with a lemon-scented oil and flashed under the grill so it is barely cooked, leaving it moist and delicate.

---

2 strips of lemon zest
85 ml (3 fl oz) extra virgin olive
  oil
675 g (1½ lb) salmon fillet, with
  skin

sea salt and black pepper
3 heaped teaspoons finely
  chopped fresh dill

Steep the strips of lemon zest in the olive oil for at least 1 hour. The salmon should be well chilled. Slice it as thinly as possible as though slicing smoked salmon, and remove the brown flesh close to the skin.

Preheat the grill. Arrange the salmon in a single layer on dinner plates. Brush with the the lemon-flavoured oil and season. Flash under the hot grill for 1 minute or less. Scatter ½ teaspoon dill over each plate.

Warm Salad of New Potatoes, Oysters and Chervil

Serves 4

Pacific (rock) oysters are available all year round. Although not as highly regarded as native oysters, they are actually preferable for this recipe – natives would be lost in a salad like this. If you don't have a mild olive oil, use half olive and half groundnut oil.

---

900 g (2 lb) medium-size new
  potatoes
24 Pacific oysters
1½ tablespoons Champagne or
  white wine vinegar
sea salt and black pepper

6 tablespoons extra virgin olive
  oil
3 heaped tablespoons coarsely
  chopped fresh chervil
  leaves

Scrub or peel the potatoes and cook in a large pan of boiling salted water until tender. Drain and leave to cool for 5 minutes. While the potatoes are cooking, shuck the oysters, pick over the meat and strain the juices into a small saucepan, discarding the last spoonful of gritty liquor. Reduce by half. To make the dressing, whisk the vinegar with seasoning, then add the oil.

Slice the warm potatoes and arrange on 4 plates. Poach the oysters in the reduced liquor for 30 seconds on each side, and place them on top of the potatoes. Add the vinaigrette to the oyster juices and spoon over the salad. Scatter the chervil over and serve.

Mushroom Caviar

Serves 4

In an ideal world you should eat this with buckwheat blinis, dripping with melted butter, but deliciously thin slices of melba toast grilled to a golden crispness are next best. If you want to jazz this up, it goes particularly well with smoked eel, as well as on toast with a poached egg on top.

---

2 tablespoons groundnut oil
2 shallots, peeled and finely
  chopped
900 g (2 lb) mushrooms,
  coarsely chopped
sea salt and black pepper

3 heaped teaspoons finely
  chopped fresh dill
2 tablespoons crème
  fraîche
lemon juice

Use two frying pans: heat some groundnut oil in each one and cook the shallots for 1 minute, then add the mushrooms, season and cook for 5–10 minutes. Initially they will throw out all their liquid, so continue to cook until they are dry. Turn into the bowl of a food processor. Process the mushrooms so they are finely chopped. Remove to a bowl and cool.

Stir in the dill and crème fraîche, adjust seasoning and add lemon juice to taste. Serve at room temperature.

Asparagus with Fried Crumbs

Serves 4

As every cook knows, there are few easier starters than fresh asparagus, but somehow serving it alone with butter rarely seems enough at a dinner party, so here it is suitably enlivened. You could, in fact, fry the crumbs in advance and reheat them.

---

675 g (1½ lb) asparagus
40 g (1½ oz) unsalted butter
4 anchovy fillets, chopped
1 clove garlic, peeled and finely
  chopped
4 heaped tablespoons white
  breadcrumbs
2 heaped teaspoons capers,
  rinsed and coarsely chopped

2 tablespoons finely chopped
  fresh flat-leaf parsley
finely grated zest of 1 lemon
black pepper

To serve
knob of unsalted butter
sea salt

Bring a large pan of salted water to the boil. Trim the aspara-gus spears where they become visibly woody. If the spears are thick then peel them to within 2.5 cm (1 inch) of the tip. Have all the other ingredients prepared and to hand.

Five minutes before you want to eat, put the asparagus on to boil. Heat the butter in a frying pan, add the anchovies and garlic, and mash to a coarse paste. Add the breadcrumbs and cook, stirring, until they are just turning golden and crisp – they will continue to cook off the heat, so remove them straightaway. Stir in the remaining ingredients.

The asparagus should cook for 4–5 minutes, it is ready when the thickest part slices with ease. Drain it, toss with the knob of butter and season with salt and pepper. Serve sprinkled with the crumb mixture.

New Potatoes 'en Papillote' with Truffles

Serves 6

Finding oneself in possession of a black Périgord truffle is more fantasy than reality, but they do exist and it does happen on occasions. The best way of enjoying them is to marry them with something really basic like potatoes or scrambled eggs. Here the truffle is cooked in a sealed packet with potatoes: these cook to a melting softness and are infused with the truffle scent.

Be sure to use real black Périgord truffles – not to be confused with the Italian summer truffle which can be found preserved in jars. (These are sometimes used by dog handlers to tempt stubborn hounds around the ring, which may be the best use for them. They do not taste of anything, let alone truffles.)

---

900 g (2 lb) small new potatoes
55 g (2 oz) unsalted butter
coarse-grain sea salt and black
  pepper

25 g (1 oz) Périgord truffle,
  finely chopped

Peel the potatoes, cut into pieces a little larger than the size of a walnut and rinse. Cut 6 rectangles of baking parchment, each 23 x 30 cm (9 x 12 inches), and butter one side. Preheat the oven to 180°C (fan oven)/190°C (375°F) gas 5.

Divide the potatoes among the pieces of paper, buttered side uppermost. Dot with more butter, season with salt and pepper and scatter chopped truffle over. Fold the edges of paper together to make neat, airtight packages and bake for 25 minutes.

Porcini Salad

Serves 4

I was served this salad at a curious restaurant called Chiesa at Trento in northern Italy. The restaurant is best known for its six-course apple menu, the Mela Party; this salad was slotted in as light relief somewhere along the way. Small and tender porcini are one of the few wild mushrooms that are good eaten raw.

---

350 g (12 oz) fresh porcini, about 6 cm (2½ inches) tall
3 tablespoons extra virgin olive oil

3 tablespoons groundnut oil
sea salt and black pepper
2 teaspoons finely chopped fresh flat-leaf parsley

Scrape the porcini clean with a knife. Just before serving the salad, slice them thinly – a mandoline will help. To avoid breaking the slices, toss them gently with the oils, seasoning and parsley, and serve straightaway.

MAIN COURSES

Vegetarian

Mushroom Fricassee with Lapsang Souchong

Serves 4

The smoky scent of Lapsang Souchong tea is a perfect match for the woody scent of wild mushrooms. Joel Antunes, formerly chef of the Michelin-starred London restaurant Les Saveurs, once cooked me a fricassee of wild mushrooms in a creamy broth flavoured with Lapsang Souchong; this is what inspired the following recipe. Use any mixture of mushrooms – I use part wild and part cultivated ones. As this dish is half stew and half soup serve it accordingly, with bread or boiled potatoes.

400 ml (14 fl oz) vegetable
   stock
3/4 teaspoon Lapsang Souchong
   tea leaves
100 g (3½ oz) unsalted butter
800 g (1¾ lb) mushrooms
3/4 teaspoon five-spice
   powder

3/4 teaspoon ground ginger
sea salt and black pepper
1 level tablespoon finely
   chopped fresh coriander
   to garnish

Put the oven on at a low heat and warm 4 bowls for serving. Bring the vegetable stock to the boil in a saucepan, pour it over the tea leaves in a bowl or jug, and leave to infuse for 5 minutes. Strain and reserve the liquid.

Clarify 70 g (2½ oz) of the butter: melt it in a saucepan over a low heat, skim off the surface foam and decant the clear yellow liquid; discard the milk solids at the bottom. Pick over and wipe the mushrooms. Trim and slice, or tear them if they are large.

Fry the mushrooms in batches to avoid overcrowding the pan (using two pans simultaneously will speed things up). Heat some of the clarified butter in each pan, add some five-spice and ginger, then the mushrooms and seasoning. Fry for 3–4 minutes. Remove to a bowl and keep warm in the oven while you cook the remainder.

Place 2 heaped tablespoons of the cooked mushrooms in a blender with the infused stock and the remaining 25 g (1 oz) of butter, and purée. Heat this sauce through in a saucepan and adjust seasoning. Serve the mushrooms in the warmed bowls with the sauce poured over and sprinkled with chopped coriander.

Filo Tart of Goat's Cheese, Spinach and Pistachios*

Serves 4

Similar to spanikopita, the Greek spinach pie, this recipe is based on a tart I ate at Ransome's Dock. The lunch was memorable, not least because it was one of those extraordinary hot summer days when you happened to find yourself beside the Thames, under an umbrella with a glass of chilled white wine. The tart was the icing on the cake.

I suspect that if I timed the preparation of this tart it would be pushing it on the 30-minute rule, but the beauty is that it can be reheated. I find if I'm entertaining as a lone hostess this makes for a very easy life – in fact, I often make this for lunch parties. Serve an interesting vegetable salad to start with.

---

175 g (6 oz) unsalted butter
675 g (1½ lb) young spinach
   leaves
55 g (2 oz) parsley leaves
sea salt and black pepper

200 g (7 oz) filo pastry
85 g (3 oz) shelled pistachio
   nuts, finely chopped
280 g (10 oz) soft, mild goat's
   cheese

Clarify the butter by melting it gently, skimming off the surface foam and decanting the clear yellow liquid; discard the milk solids on the bottom. Wash the spinach in plenty of water and shake it thoroughly dry. Heat a little clarified butter in a frying pan, add some of the spinach leaves and parsley, season and cook, tossing them, until they have wilted. Remove with any juices to a bowl and cook the remaining spinach and parsley: you will need to do this in several batches and should only use up to about 25 g (1 oz) of butter in the process. Drain all the cooked spinach in a sieve, pressing out as much of the juice as possible.

Take a 23 x 30 cm (9 x 12 inch) ovenproof dish, 5 cm (2 inches) deep, and brush it with clarified butter. Layer half the pastry in the dish, painting each sheet with clarified butter and scattering half the chopped nuts on the pastry halfway through. Arrange the spinach and goat's cheese evenly over the surface. Layer the remaining pastry on top, again painting each sheet with butter and scattering on the remaining pistachios halfway through.

Preheat the oven to 200°C (fan oven)/220°C (425°F) gas 7 and bake for 25–35 minutes. The pastry should be quite a deep gold – don't remove it as soon as the pastry starts colouring on top, because the bottom pastry may still be raw. You can cook the tart in advance and reheat it if required.

Fish

Monkfish Bourride

Serves 4

Bourride has great finesse and fares well when reproduced on foreign shores. Any firm-fleshed white fish can be used: sea bass, turbot, brill or John Dory can replace monkfish, and shellfish are a welcome addition.

For the aïoli
sea salt
8 small cloves garlic, peeled and chopped
2 egg yolks (size 2)
75 ml (2½ fl oz) extra virgin olive oil
75 ml (2½ fl oz) groundnut oil
1 teaspoon lemon juice

For the croutons
12 x 12.5 cm (½ inch) slices of French bread
olive oil
1 clove garlic

For the base
1.3 kg (3 lb) monkfish (weight including skin and central bone)
300 ml (½ pint) fish stock
150 ml (¼ pint) white wine
2 shallots, peeled and finely chopped
1 leek, sliced
55 g (2 oz) fennel, finely chopped
strip of orange peel, 5 cm x 5 mm (2 x ¼ inch)
bouquet garni of bay, thyme and parsley
sea salt and black pepper
20 saffron filaments, ground and infused with 1 tbsp boiling water
finely chopped fresh parsley

Sprinkle a little salt over the garlic and crush to a paste using the flat edge of a knife. Whisk the egg yolks and garlic together in a large bowl. Gradually add the oils, then stir in the lemon juice. Set the aïoli aside.

Shallow fry the French bread slices in olive oil until golden; they should be more like fried bread than crisp biscuits. Rub each crouton with the halved garlic clove.

Remove the monkfish from the central bone and skin it. Cutting on the bias, slice fillets 2.5 cm (1 inch) thick and season. Place the stock, wine, vegetables, orange peel, bouquet garni and seasoning into a large saucepan and bring to the boil. Cover and simmer for 10 minutes. Add the fish to the pan, bring back to a simmer and cook, covered, for 3–4 minutes, until the fish is firm.

Using a slotted spoon, remove the fish and vegetables to a warm serving dish or bowls, discarding herbs and peel. Add the saffron tincture to the broth.

Pour the broth on to the aïoli, mixing, return to pan and thicken without boiling. Strain the broth over the fish and vegetables. Sprinkle with finely chopped parsley and serve with the croutons.

Rick Stein's Mouclade

Serves 4

A gorgeous dish of mussels in their salty juices, flavoured with curry spices and enriched with crème fraîche. This main-course version is lavish, with pieces of turbot, plaice and cod nestling between the mussels. Boiled potatoes or French bread complete the picture.

---

900 g (2 lb) mussels
50 ml (2 fl oz) dry white wine
25 g (1 oz) unsalted butter
115 g (4 oz) white and pale
 green parts of leeks, sliced
 into thin 5 cm (2 inch)
 strips
55 g (2 oz) onion, finely
 chopped
1 clove garlic, peeled and finely
 chopped
1 tablespoon Cognac
good pinch of saffron
 filaments
scant ¼ teaspoon curry
 powder

150 ml (¼ pint) crème fraîche
225 g (8 oz) each turbot, cod
 and monkfish fillet, cut into
 4 pieces
sea salt and black pepper
150 ml (¼ pint) double
 strength fish stock
1 rounded teaspoon beurre
 manié (equal quantities of
 unsalted butter and plain
 flour mashed together)
finely chopped fresh chives to
 garnish

Wash the mussels in several changes of cold water. Scrape away any barnacles and pull out the beards, discarding mussels that are broken or do not close when tapped sharply, then wash again. Place the mussels and wine in a large saucepan, cover and cook over a high heat until the shells open, 3–4 minutes. Drain in a colander set in a bowl, reserving the liquor. Shell three-quarters of the mussels. Place shelled and unshelled together in a dish and cover. You can prepare everything in advance to this point, and it will only take 15 minutes to finish.

Melt the butter in the mussel saucepan, add the vegetables, Cognac and spices and cook gently until soft, about 5 minutes. Warm a large serving dish in a low oven. Add the mussel liquor to the pan (discard the last tablespoon of liquor, which will be gritty). Add the crème fraîche and heat to just below boiling. Place the fish fillets on top of the vegetables, season lightly, cover and braise the fish until just cooked, 4–6 minutes. Remove the fish to the warm serving dish and cover with foil. Add the stock and beurre manié to the pan and simmer for 3–4 minutes. Adjust seasoning – it should be slightly salty – and add the mussels to heat through. Pour the mussels and sauce over the fish, sprinkle with chives and serve.

Mohammed's Fish Tagine*

Serves 4

The coastline around Essaouira is famous for its fish tagines, but they had eluded us after a day spent searching during a trip to Morocco. Returning across the deserted plains to Marrakesh, we arrived at a small café that grandly announced itself as 'auberge-restaurant-bar'. Touali Mohammed, the chef, seemed delighted to deviate from the quasi-French menu, and cooked us the most spectacular sea bass tagine. Both grey mullet and sea bass are excellent here.

6 tablespoons extra virgin olive oil
25 filaments saffron
2 teaspoons paprika
2 teaspoons ground cumin
1 tablespoon tomato purée
1 onion, halved and sliced
1 large clove garlic, peeled and finely chopped
2 green peppers, cored, deseeded and cut into strips

350 g (12 oz) main crop potatoes
sea salt and black pepper
1 x 1.3 kg (3 lb) grey mullet, gutted and cleaned
450 g (1 lb) beefsteak tomatoes, skinned and thickly sliced
3 lemon slices
85 ml (3 fl oz) white wine

Heat 4 tablespoons of the oil in a flameproof casserole large enough to hold the fish, add the spices and immediately turn the heat down low. Add the tomato purée, onion and garlic and cook for 2–3 minutes. Add the peppers and cook for a further 8–9 minutes until they soften a little, stirring frequently. Distribute this mixture evenly over the bottom of the casserole.

Preheat the oven to 200°C (fan oven)/220°C (425°F) gas 7. Peel and thinly slice the potatoes, and lay them on top of the peppers. Season. Place the fish on top, then the tomatoes, then the lemon, seasoning each layer. Pour the wine and remaining olive oil over. Cover with foil, or a lid, and bake for 30 minutes. Uncover and cook for a further 20 minutes. Discard the lemon, and fillet the fish as you serve it, accompanied by the vegetables and sauce.

Roast Mackerel with Sweet and Sour Tomato Sauce

Serves 4

I think mackerel is a very under-rated fish. Its flesh is rich and oily and is beautifully partnered here by a sweet but tart tomato sauce and a sprinkling of coriander. I would serve new potatoes roasted in their skins with this, but if you need something quicker then rice will do.

4 mackerel, cleaned, head and tails removed
sea salt and black pepper
chopped fresh coriander to garnish

For the sauce
1 kg (2¼ lb) plum tomatoes
4 tablespoons extra virgin olive oil
2 cloves garlic, peeled and finely chopped
2 level teaspoons finely chopped fresh red chilli
2 heaped teaspoons caster sugar
2 tablespoons balsamic vinegar

Preheat the oven to 200°C (fan oven)/220°C (425°F) gas 7. Bring a large pan of water to the boil. Cut out a cone from the top of each tomato. Plunge them into the boiling water for 30 seconds and then into a sink of cold water; slip off the skins and slice thickly.

Score the mackerel diagonally at 2.5 cm (1 inch) intervals and place in a roasting dish. Season on both sides and roast for 15–20 minutes.

Heat the olive oil in a large saucepan, add the garlic and chilli and moments later add the tomatoes. Cook for a minute or two. Season, add the sugar and vinegar and cook until reduced to a thickish sauce, 7–10 minutes. Adjust seasoning.

Spoon the sauce over the whole mackerel and sprinkle with coriander.

Mussel Risotto with Basil Cream*

Serves 6

A risotto takes full advantage of salty mussel juices. But should you think that by becoming acquainted with arborio that you have mastered the risotto, then you may have to think again. Three types of rice are now available in good delis. Carnaroli pulls rank over arborio with its big, fat grains; they are both superfino grades, but grains of carnaroli are firm and distinct when cooked. Vialone nano, a fino grade, is very elegant and completes the trio: its short grains cook to a delectable consistency without turning to pudding.

---

4 heaped tablespoons crème fraîche
20 g (3/4 oz) basil leaves
sea salt
1.8 kg (4 lb) mussels, cleaned
300 ml (1/2 pint) white wine
1.2 litres (2 pints) vegetable stock
85 g (3 oz) unsalted butter
1 onion, peeled and finely chopped

425 g (15 oz) risotto rice, ideally carnaroli
25 saffron filaments, ground and infused with 2 tablespoons boiling stock
55 g (2 oz) Parmesan, freshly grated
115 g (4 oz) young spinach leaves
black pepper

Liquidise the crème fraîche and basil leaves, and season with salt. Place the mussels and wine in a large saucepan, cover and steam for 4–5 minutes over a high heat until the shells open. Shell the mussels, reserving all the juices. Keep the stock at a simmer while cooking the risotto. Heat the butter in the mussel pan and sweat the onion until soft and translucent. Add the rice and cook for 1–2 minutes. Add the mussel juices, in two lots, and the saffron. Once these have been absorbed start to add the stock, a ladleful at a time. It will take about 25 minutes in total to cook the risotto; the rice should be firm to the bite.

Stir in the Parmesan, toss in the spinach leaves to wilt and add the shelled mussels to heat through. Adjust seasoning. Serve the risotto with a dollop of basil cream in the centre, allowing it to melt over the top.

Grilled Lobster with Garlic Butter

Serves 2

This is the upmarket version of prawns with garlic butter. Sweet lobster flesh dripping with rich, garlicky juices is positively sensational.

---

2 x 550 g (1¼ lb) live lobsters

For the garlic butter
**55 g (2 oz) unsalted butter,
    softened**
**1 large clove garlic, peeled and
    crushed to a paste with salt**

**1 heaped tablespoon finely
    chopped fresh flat-leaf
    parsley**

To serve
watercress sprigs
French bread

Blend all the ingredients for the garlic butter and reserve. Bring a large pan of salted water to the boil: it should be almost as salty as seawater. Plunge the live lobsters into the pan, cover with the lid and cook for 5 minutes. Remove them and, once cool enough to handle, break off the claws and split the body down the centre with a large knife, starting at the head end. Remove the brown meat and reserve for another use. Remove and discard the stomach (the dark tract running along the tail section). Remove the body flesh in one piece and rinse the shell if it is messy.

Smear some of the garlic butter inside the shell and return the lobster flesh with the curved, pink side uppermost. Crack the claws (I use a marble rolling-pin) and pull out the claw meat in one piece; lay this in the cavity where the brown meat was. Smear the remaining garlic butter over the lobster meat. All this can be done in advance.

Preheat the grill. Grill the lobster for 5 minutes, and serve with a few watercress sprigs and lots of crusty French bread.

Warm Salad of Poached Salmon, Baby Spinach and Asparagus with a Balsamic Dressing

Serves 4

---

1 tablespoon balsamic vinegar
sea salt and black pepper
6 tablespoons extra virgin olive oil
unsalted butter
4 x 115 g (4 oz) salmon fillets, skinned
fish stock

2 sprigs fresh tarragon
200 g (7 oz) asparagus, trimmed
175 g (6 oz) baby spinach leaves
1 large beefsteak tomato, skinned, deseeded and diced

Whisk the balsamic vinegar with seasoning and add the oil. Preheat the oven to 200°C (fan oven)/220°C (425°F) gas 7.

Butter a shallow baking dish. Place the salmon fillets in it, season and add fish stock to a depth of 5 mm (1/4 inch). Add the tarragon sprigs. Cover with foil and bake for 14 minutes (if you have a very hot oven the salmon may be ready in 10 minutes – check it).

Meanwhile, boil the asparagus in salted water until just cooked; drain and season with salt. Toss the warm asparagus, spinach and tomato with the vinaigrette. Place a pile on each plate. Lay a piece of salmon on top and drizzle over a little of the cooking juices. Serve immediately.

Oysters with a Champagne Sabayon and Herbed Noodles

Serves 6

The only irksome part of this dish is the shucking of the oysters, the answer being to appoint a shucker.

---

36 Pacific (rock) oysters	cayenne pepper
2 egg yolks (size 2)	450 g (1 lb) fresh tagliolini
50 ml (2 fl oz) Champagne	sea salt
175 g (6 oz) unsalted butter, melted	2 heaped tablespoons finely chopped fresh chervil

---

Shuck the oysters and place them in a bowl. Pour the juices from the shells into a saucepan and reduce to 2 small tablespoons of liquor. Place 3 deep shell halves on the outside of each plate. Pick over the oysters to remove any bits of shell. Whisk together the egg yolks and Champagne in a double boiler until you have a stable sabayon several times the original volume. The froth should be hot but bearable to your finger's touch. Gradually whisk in 140 g (5 oz) of the melted butter and the reduced oyster juices to taste. Season with a suspicion of cayenne pepper.

While making the sauce, boil the tagliolini; dress with the remaining melted butter, season with salt and mix in the chervil. Heat the oysters in a saucepan for about 1 minute until they turn opaque and firm up slightly. Do not cook them.

Place the oysters in the half-shells and spoon over the sabayon. With a fork make a nest of noodles and place in the centre of each plate.

Meat

Coq au Vin*

Serves 4

One Sunday I opened my *Observer* for my weekly instalment of Nigel Slater, cook extraordinaire, and there accompanied by his typically mouthwatering visuals was a blow by blow account of coq au vin. Thank heavens someone had had the good sense to reinstate this 70s bistro cliché.

It's everything that Floyd purports to be: a wall of flames as you flambé the brandy, followed up with a bottle of red wine – pour it in without actually looking for maximum aplomb. The result is a casserole of glistening, dark red sauce, and golden pieces of chicken, perfumed with a few bay leaves and thyme sprigs.

I have not stuck rigorously to the authentic version, but it is here in essence: I have added dried porcini instead of bacon, though you could add bacon when frying the onions. I like to serve this with baked or boiled potatoes, something to mash into the juices.

This does not conform to a 30-minute rule, but it can be made in advance and will accommodate numbers if you want to cook it in quantity.

10 g (¼ oz) dried porcini	1 tablespoon brandy
2 tablespoons extra virgin olive oil	1 bottle red wine
	3 bay leaves
2 onions, peeled and chopped	3 sprigs fresh thyme
1.3 kg (3 lb) chicken pieces	25 g (1 oz) unsalted butter
plain flour seasoned with sea salt and black pepper	225 g (8 oz) button mushrooms

Cover the dried porcini with boiling water and soak for 15 minutes. Heat the olive oil in a large saucepan and sweat the onions over a moderate heat for 8–12 minutes until they are turning golden, stirring regularly. Remove to a bowl. Turn the chicken pieces in the seasoned flour and cook until they are nicely coloured on both sides: you will have to do this in two lots.

Return all the chicken and the onions to the pan. Heat the brandy in a spoon or a ladle, ignite (you can do this by placing it very near a gas flame) and pour it over the chicken – try to pour it over gradually to avoid the flames shooting up. Pour in the red wine, add the herbs and porcini with their soaking liquor and bring to a simmer. Cover and cook over a gentle heat for 40 minutes.

Remove the chicken. Skim any surface fat and boil the liquor until it has reduced by half. Melt the butter in a frying pan and sauté the mushrooms whole until golden on all sides; season them. Return the chicken to the saucepan together with the mushrooms and simmer for a further 15 minutes. Adjust seasoning before serving.

Chicken Baked in Salt with Lapsang Souchong*

Serves 4

This is a foolproof method of ensuring beautifully moist, tea-scented flesh. It also looks stunning in its white crystalline coat speckled with black. Serve with a salad of sliced avocado and watercress dressed with a balsamic vinaigrette.

---

1 kg (2¼ lb) fine crystal sea salt

4 heaped tablespoons Lapsang Souchong tea leaves

1 x 1.6 kg (3½ lb) oven-ready free-range chicken

Preheat the oven to 200°C (fan oven)/220°C (425°F) gas 7 and line a baking tray with foil. Mix the salt and tea together in a large bowl and add 250 ml (9 fl oz) of cold water. Blend to a firm paste. Lay half of this on the foil as a base for the chicken. Pierce the chicken all over with a knife or skewer and place it on top. Pat the remainder of the salt mixture around it, so the chicken is coated to a thickness of about 8 mm (3/8 inch). Bake for 1 hour.

Allow to stand for 15 minutes, then break off the salt crust, which will have dried out, before carving. Serve hot or cold.

Roast Goose with Port and Shallot Marmalade*

Serves 4

This port and shallot marmalade provides the sweetness so agreeable with goose. Combined with a crispy, rich skin, a tender, dark flesh and a thin gravy, it is very special. Save the dripping and you can live off sensational roast potatoes for months afterwards; even fried eggs on toast are elevated to gourmet status when fried in goose fat.

1 goose
groundnut oil
sea salt and black pepper

1 level teaspoon sugar
1 level teaspoon sea salt
1/8 teaspoon black pepper
200 ml (7 fl oz) port

For the marmalade
1 teaspoon olive oil
675 g (1½ lb) shallots or
   onions, or a mixture of the
   two, peeled and thinly sliced

To make the marmalade, heat the olive oil in a saucepan, add the shallots or onions, sugar, salt and pepper and cook, covered, over a low heat for 35 minutes, stirring occasionally. Add the port and simmer, uncovered, for another 30–35 minutes, again stirring occasionally, until you have a thick, syrupy marmalade. Serve at room temperature.

Preheat the oven to 200°C (fan oven)/220°C (425°F) gas 7. Place a rack in a baking tray that contains a few millimetres of water in the bottom; place a large sheet of foil on the rack and pierce so that the fat can drain through. Remove any surplus fat at the entrance to the body cavity of the goose. Fill with a stuffing if desired. Rub with oil and season, and prick the skin and fat gland under each wing. Cover the legs with some surplus fat. Place the goose breast-side up on the foil and wrap it into a parcel. Cover the legs with a second piece of foil to protect them throughout cooking.

Calculate the total cooking time at 15–17 minutes to each 450 g (1 lb). Roast the goose for one third of the cooking time, then unwrap, turn it breast down and baste well. Roast, uncovered, for another third of the cooking time. Turn breast uppermost again for the remainder of the cooking time, leaving it uncovered and basting well. Leave the bird to rest while you make the gravy (see page 58). Serve with the marmalade.

Tea-smoked Duck Breasts with Pineapple and Date Salsa*

Serves 4

Serve this cold with salads or hot with spinach sautéed in sesame oil and soy sauce, scattered with toasted sesame seeds. Salads, too, should have an oriental touch. I have cooked this with both Gunpowder and Lapsang Souchong tea, but Oolong and Keemun would also work well.

---

4 duck breasts
4 teaspoons light soy sauce
sea salt and black pepper

For the smoking mixture
3 heaped tablespoons Gun-
powder tea leaves
3 heaped tablespoons white
rice
3 heaped tablespoons brown
sugar

For the salsa
140 g (5 oz) dates
175 g (6 oz) fresh pineapple,
diced into 5 mm (¼ inch)
cubes
2 teaspoons finely chopped
shallots
2 tablespoons lime juice
½ teaspoon toasted and
ground cumin seed

Score the fat on the duck breasts at 2.5 cm (1 inch) intervals. Rub the soy sauce over each one and season on both sides. Line a wok or a steamer with foil. Mix together the tea leaves, rice and brown sugar in a bowl and scatter this over the foil. Place the duck breasts, fat side up, on a steaming rack over the smoking mixture. Cover with a lid and seal, if required, with damp tea towels to prevent any smoke from escaping.

Cook over a high heat for 4 minutes, then over a low heat for a further 20 minutes if you like duck pink, or 25 minutes if you prefer it more well-done. Leave the meat to stand for 15 minutes, then slice thinly and serve with the salsa.

While the duck is cooking prepare the salsa. Skin, halve and stone the dates. Cut into 5 mm (¼ inch) cubes. Mix with the remaining salsa ingredients and season.

Salad of Chicken and French Beans with a Sesame Seed Dressing

Serves 4

Typical of many Indonesian salads this does not contain any oil, which makes it perfect for healthy eating. It has a really clean, strong flavour with plenty of character.

Depending on how Eastern-orientated your local supermarket is you may need to buy the ketjap manis (a sweet soy sauce) and the sake from a specialist oriental deli. You could, though, substitute Kikkoman soy sauce for the ketjap manis and sweeten it with a little molasses or muscovado sugar.

---

450 ml (¾ pint) chicken stock
sea salt and black pepper
3 chicken breasts, boned and
    skinned
400 g (14 oz) French beans

3 tablespoons white sesame
    seeds
2 tablespoons ketjap manis
2 tablespoons sake

Bring the chicken stock to the boil in a medium-size saucepan and season it. Add the chicken breasts. Bring the stock back to a simmer, then cover and poach for 12–15 minutes. Remove and cool; reserve the stock. Slice the breasts in half horizontally and then into long thin strips, cutting across the grain.

Bring a large pan of salted water to the boil. Top and tail the beans and halve if very long, then boil for 3–5 minutes until just cooked. Drain and refresh in cold water.

Toast the sesame seeds in a dry frying pan until they start to darken, then finely grind three-quarters of them in an electric coffee grinder or spice mill. Mix the ground seeds in a bowl with the ketjap manis, sake and 2 tablespoons of the chicken stock.

Place the beans in a bowl and mix with the dressing. Save a few sesame seeds to sprinkle over the finished salad, and just before serving toss the chicken slices and the remainder of the seeds into the beans. Adjust seasoning and serve.

Braised Partridge with Juniper Berries and Girolles*

Serves 6

Grey partridges are smaller, rarer and more tender than red-legged French birds. Braise them with juniper berries, accentuated with a hint of gin, and accompany with some pan-fried girolles. You can cut the legs and breasts off each bird before serving to assure neat eating, but this isn't essential. A creamy gratin of butternut squash with garlic makes the perfect accompaniment, as does a celeriac purée.

---

6 grey partridges, trussed
sea salt and black pepper
2 tablespoons groundnut oil
70 g (2½ oz) unsalted butter
175 g (6 oz) mixed celery,
   carrot and leek, chopped
2 tablespoons gin
175 ml (6 fl oz) red wine
450 ml (¾ pint) strong chicken
   stock

2 teaspoons crushed juniper
   berries
4 cloves
2 sprigs fresh thyme
2 cloves garlic, peeled and
   chopped
350 g (12 oz) girolles, cleaned
   and sliced

Preheat the oven to 200°C (fan oven)/220°C (425°F) gas 7. Season the partridges. Heat the groundnut oil with 15 g (½ oz) butter in a heavy-bottomed casserole and sear the birds on all sides until they colour, then remove them. Do this in two lots. Add the chopped vegetables and cook until lightly coloured. Warm the gin in a ladle, ignite and pour over the vegetables; add the wine, stock, spices, thyme and garlic. Return the birds to the casserole and bring to the boil, then cover and cook in the oven for 30 minutes; the birds' juices should be clear and slightly pink, but not bloody.

Strain the cooking juices into a small saucepan, skim off any fat and reduce by half. Before serving, heat through and whisk in

25 g (1 oz) butter. Keep the birds in the covered casserole for 10 minutes before serving. Remove each breast with the leg. If not serving straightaway you can prepare the dish to this point in advance and return to the oven to reheat.

Heat the remaining 25 g (1 oz) of butter in a frying pan and sauté the girolles over a high heat for 3 minutes until starting to colour; season. Serve the partridges and mushrooms with the sauce poured over.

Salad of Puy Lentils with Salami

Serves 4

---

2 tablespoons red wine vinegar	2 tablespoons finely chopped
black pepper	fresh chives
1 clove garlic, peeled and	225 g (8 oz) Puy lentils
crushed to a paste with salt	85 g (3 oz) young spinach
8 tablespoons extra virgin olive	leaves
oil	140 g (5 oz) sliced salami, rind
	removed

Whisk the vinegar with pepper and garlic. Add the oil and the chives. Boil the lentils in water for 25 minutes; add the spinach 30 seconds before the end of the cooking just to blanch it. Drain the lentils and spinach and allow to cool.

Toss the lentils and spinach with the dressing and arrange with the salami on a large plate, or plates. Serve at room temperature.

Desserts

Vanilla Ice-Cream

Serves 4

Yes I'm afraid you do need an ice-cream maker for this one. But, as I explained in the Introduction, this is one of the best investments you can make as far as producing 'fast and fantastic' puddings can go.

---

1 vanilla pod
2 eggs (size 2)
70 g (2½ oz) caster sugar
350 ml (12 fl oz) double cream

175 ml (6 fl oz) milk
1 teaspoon orange flower water
  (optional)

Slit the vanilla pod, open it and scrape out the seeds by running a knife along the inside; cut up the pod. Place both seeds and pod in a blender with the remaining ingredients and liquidise. Pass through a sieve and freeze according to manufacturer's instructions for your ice-cream maker.

Ideally, eat straightaway without a spell in the freezer: the consistency is a world apart from ice-cream that has been frozen.

Zabaglione Mousse

Serves 4

Please, please don't be put off making zabaglione, because it is incredibly quick and easy. Here I have turned it into a mousse, so you get the full benefit of that fiery froth, combined with the convenience of pulling it out of the fridge at the last minute. Serve this with chocolate thins or dessert biscuits.

---

1 heaped teaspoon powdered gelatine	125 ml (4 fl oz) Marsala
4 egg yolks (size 2)	200 ml (7 fl oz) double cream
55 g (2 oz) caster sugar	140 g (5 oz) fromage frais

Sprinkle the gelatine over 1 tablespoon of boiling water and leave for 4 minutes, then stir to dissolve. (If necessary, stand it inside another bowl of boiling water and give it a bit longer.)

Bring about 2.5 cm (1 inch) of water to the boil in a small saucepan or the bottom half of a double boiler. In a heatproof bowl, or the top half of the boiler, whisk the egg yolks and caster sugar together over the boiling water to warm them through. Now whisk in the Marsala, a little at a time, and continue whisking until the mixture is thick and frothy and makes a ribbon, having multiplied several times in volume. Be careful not to overcook it, otherwise it will turn grainy. Remove from the boiling water and continue whisking for a minute or two until the mixture has cooled a tad. Remove it to a large bowl.

Whip the double cream in a bowl until it is stiff. Whisk the fromage frais into the zabaglione, then the double cream. Fold the gelatine solution into the mousse. Pour into a bowl or glasses, cover with clingfilm and leave to set in the fridge for several hours or overnight.

Joyce Molyneux's Saffron and Honey Custard*

Serves 4

Joyce Molyneux serves this delightful creation at The Carved Angel in Dartmouth. The original version calls for quinces, though she suggests rhubarb, gooseberries or stone fruit such as plums or damsons in their place. The richness of the custard is offset by the tartness of the fruit. Sweet recipes calling for saffron are not that common, which makes this an unusual offering.

450 g (1 lb) gooseberries, topped and tailed	For the custard
115 g (4 oz) caster sugar	600 ml (1 pint) single cream
1 vanilla pod	15 saffron filaments, ground
150 ml (¼ pint) water	6 egg yolks (size 2)
	55 g (2 oz) clear honey

Place the gooseberries in a pan with the sugar, vanilla pod and water. Poach for 30 minutes until the juices are thick and syrupy. Remove the vanilla pod, and spoon the fruit into ramekins.

Preheat the oven to 140°C (fan oven)/150°C (300°F) gas 2. Heat the cream with the saffron. Whisk the egg yolks and honey together, blend with the cream and cook over a gentle heat until the custard thickens. Strain and pour over fruit. Bake in a bain marie for 1 hour. Eat warm or cold.

Granita di Caffè with Cognac Cream

Serves 4

Do as the Italians do and and have this after lunch on a stifling afternoon: half drink and half sorbet, it will numb your mouth by the time you have finished it. Cognac adds dimension. Accompany the granita with marrons glacés or some syrupy Middle Eastern pastries.

---

85 g (3 oz) caster sugar	**To serve**
450 ml (¾ pint) espresso coffee	**300 ml (½ pint) double cream**
	1 tablespoon Cognac

Dissolve the sugar in the coffee while it is hot, then let it cool. Pour into a shallow container and place in the freezer. It is impossible to predict exactly how long a granita will take to freeze; this depends on the freezer. The important thing is to churn it regularly. Assuming it will take 3 hours, stir it every 20 minutes: as crystals freeze around the outside of the tray scrape them into the centre and mash it up thoroughly. Once it has frozen it will be good to eat for a couple of hours beyond this, but should not be left indefinitely.

Whip the cream with the Cognac. Serve the granita in glasses with a generous spoonful of Cognac cream on top.

Apple Gratin with Tamarillos*

Serves 6

Apples offset the tartness of the tamarillos: serve it with vanilla ice-cream for the perfect finale.

1.5 kg (3 lb 6 oz) dessert apples	**6 tamarillos**
40 g (1½ oz) caster sugar	**3 egg whites (size 2)**
squeeze of lemon juice	**icing sugar for dusting**
2 teaspoons Calvados (optional)	

Quarter the apples and place in a saucepan with the sugar and 6 tablespoons of water. Cover and simmer for 30 minutes, stirring occasionally. Transfer the apples to a food processor and purée. Sieve the purée, then add the lemon juice and Calvados and allow to cool. Peel and slice the tamarillos.

Just before serving, preheat the grill. Whisk the egg whites until stiff and fold into the purée. Spread over the bottom of six heatproof dessert plates or one large platter. Arrange the tamarillo slices on top, pressing them gently into the purée, then dust liberally with sifted icing sugar. Grill until golden in places. Serve straightaway.

Sauternes Jelly with Winter Fruits

Serves 6

This is as close as you'll get to divine trifle, and the better the wine the more divine it is. This jelly is decidedly alcoholic: make a separate children's version using apple juice if necessary.

Silver leaf costs a fraction of the price of gold; either looks exquisite. It is extremely delicate – the best way to handle it is to cut squares using scissors while it is still between the two dividing layers of tissue paper, then lay the squares in place using tweezers. The leaf is purely decorative, and can be omitted.

---

1 bottle Sauternes (75 cl)
1 sachet powdered gelatine
6 clementines
2 tablespoons pomegranate
    seeds
2 sheets gold or silver leaf, each
    9 x 9 cm (3¹/₂ x 3¹/₂ inches),
    cut into small squares

To serve
300 ml (¹/₂ pint) double or
    whipping cream, whipped

Bring 125 ml (4 fl oz) of the wine to the boil in a small saucepan; remove from the heat and sprinkle the gelatine over. Leave for a few minutes, then stir to dissolve. If the gelatine has not completely dissolved, stand the saucepan in a second saucepan of just-boiled water. Gradually add the remainder of the wine to the gelatine mixture. Pour into a jug, cover and chill overnight until it sets.

Peel the clementines, remove the pith and skin each segment with a knive; reserve.

To serve, lay out six chilled dessert plates and place some clementine segments and pomegranate seeds on each one. Lightly whisk the jelly to break it up and spoon half over the fruit. Lay a few squares of gold or silver leaf on top, then spoon over the remaining jelly. Decorate with another few squares of leaf. Top each serving with a dollop of whipped cream.

Chocolate Fudge Cake

Serves 4–6

I feel like a child returning to its first-ever recipe of rock cakes when I call up this recipe: I served it daily in my early days as a cook at Books for Cooks. It comes from an Australian book called *More Greta Anna Recipes*, which has provided me with endless inspiration. It is, I believe, the chocolate truffle-cum-fudge cake to end them all.

500 g (1 lb 2 oz) dark chocolate	4 eggs (size 2)
2½ tablespoons caster sugar	1 tablespoon plain flour
140 g (5 oz) unsalted butter	

Preheat the oven to 200°C (fan oven)/220°C (425°F) gas 7. Break up the chocolate and place in the top half of a double boiler, or in a heatproof bowl, with 1½ tablespoons of the sugar and the butter. Set over a pan of simmering water. Once melted beat the mixture until it is homogenous and well combined.

Place the eggs and remaining sugar in a food processor (you can also do this with a hand whisk) and beat for 10 minutes until the mixture is very thick and pale, and has at least doubled in volume. Fold in the flour. Drop the chocolate mixture on top of the egg mixture and combine the two as quickly as possible – if using a food processor, then a quick burst at high speed will do it.

Pour the mixture into a buttered 20 cm (8 inch) cake tin with a removable base. Bake for 10 minutes – the centre will remain unset. Loosen the cake from the side of the tin with a knife. Once the cake is cool cover it with clingfilm and chill for several hours until it is set further. Try to serve it soon after this: although it will keep for several days it sets even harder and you lose that seductive quality. Serve in small slices.

Chocolate Soufflé with Chocolate-Clove Sauce

Serves 6

I am not of the lighter-than-air school when it comes to chocolate soufflés; I like them rich and dark, heavy with chocolate and *baveuse* in the centre. Some thin almond tuiles, as found at a good French pâtisserie, will provide the elegance.

For the soufflé
unsalted butter and caster sugar for the dish
55 g (2 oz) unsalted butter
55 g (2 oz) plain flour
300 ml (1/2 pint) milk
25 g (1 oz) vanilla sugar
175 g (6 oz) dark chocolate, melted
2 tablespoons brandy or dark rum
4 egg yolks (size 2)
7 egg whites (size 2)

For the chocolate-clove sauce
250 g (9 oz) dark chocolate, broken into pieces
40 g (1½ oz) unsalted butter
50 ml (2 fl oz) milk
50 ml (2 fl oz) double cream
2 tablespoons strong black coffee
3 cloves, freshly ground

Butter the inside of a straight-sided 18 cm (7 inch) soufflé dish, or 6 individual 10 cm (4 inch) dishes, and dust with caster sugar. Melt the butter in a small saucepan, stir in the flour and cook this roux for a couple of minutes. Take off the heat and gradually incorporate the milk and vanilla sugar. Cook the sauce for 4 minutes, stirring. Remove from the heat and cool for a minute or two, then beat in the melted chocolate, alcohol and egg yolks. You can prepare the pudding to this point in advance.

To make the chocolate-clove sauce, set a heatproof bowl over a pan of simmering water; place the chocolate in the bowl with the butter and melt. Whisk in the milk, cream, coffee and cloves and warm over the simmering water. The sauce can be made in advance and refrigerated, covered, for several days.

Preheat oven to 200°C (fan oven)/220°C (425°F) gas 7. Whisk the egg whites until stiff. Stir a couple of spoonfuls into the sauce and incorporate the remainder as quickly and deftly as possible. Spoon the mixture into the soufflé dish or dishes, filling individual dishes three-quarters full. Bake, allowing plenty of headroom, giving individual soufflés 10 minutes. Bake a large soufflé for 20–25 minutes; do not open the oven door for the first 15 minutes and turn the oven down to 160°C (fan oven)/170°C (325°F) gas 3 after 5 minutes.

Serve with the hot chocolate sauce: make a hole in the centre of individual soufflés and pour it in.

Calvados Truffles*

Makes 30–40

---

175 ml (6 fl oz) double cream	2 teaspoons Calvados
280 g (10 oz) dark chocolate	good quality cocoa powder
85 g (3 oz) soft unsalted butter	

Boil the cream for 2 minutes, then cool to room temperature. Chop the chocolate into small pieces and place it in a heatproof bowl set over simmering water. Once the chocolate has melted incorporate the cream. Whisk the butter in a food processor, then add the chocolate cream and the Calvados. Leave somewhere cool, but not cold, for it to firm up.

When the mixture is firm enough to keep a spoon standing upright, beat it until smooth and pipe into cones on a baking tray lined with baking parchment. Leave in a cool place until solid, then roll in cocoa powder. Store in a cool place, but not the refrigerator.

SEASONAL DINNER PARTIES

SPRING DINNER PARTY for 6

Asparagus, prosciutto and rocket with a dried cherry vinaigrette

Chicken roasted with chilli, rosemary and cinnamon
Garlic mashed potato
Spring greens

Mango fool with bitter chocolate thins

Roast chicken is the old diamond of the British dining table, and here it is all dressed up, its juices scented with rosemary and cinnamon, redolent of Morocco, with a really rich, garlicky purée of potato to mop them up. A hard act to beat. Spring greens are strong and faintly bitter, cabbages without hearts, though purple sprouting broccoli is also an option.

Purists will argue that prosciutto should be eaten alone, some white bread and butter alongside. And this is indeed an answer if time is tight. Remember that Parma ham is just one type of air-dried ham – a variation would be to use a French Bayonne or a Spanish serrano, or buy British. Richard Woodall's 'Cumbria Mature Royal Ham' is a superb balance of sweet and salty to rival the Continent's finest: cured in ale and molasses according to a family recipe that dates back to 1843.

The mango fool is cool, pale orange, and very light, like an unset mousse. By contrast the chocolate thins are dark and crisp. Off-the-peg labels such as Lindt are fine, though more serious chocolate counters offer the couture equivalent.

Richard Woodall's Hams are available from good delicatessens or mail order: 01229 717237.

Order of Work
1. Prepare mango fool.
2. Roast chicken; prepare mash and greens while it is cooking (or prepare vegetables in advance and reheat them).
3. Make dressing and cook asparagus.
4. Let chicken rest during first course.

Asparagus, Prosciutto and Rocket with a Dried Cherry Vinaigrette

450 g (1 lb) asparagus **225 g (8 oz) prosciutto** **25 g (1 oz) rocket**	For the dressing **sea salt and black pepper** **1 tablespoon balsamic vinegar** **6 tablespoons extra virgin olive oil** **25 g (1 oz) dried cherries, coarsely chopped**

Bring a pan of salted water to the boil. Cut off the woody base of the asparagus spears, and peel to within 2.5 cm (1 inch) of the tip. Boil for 4–5 minutes, leaving it firm to the bite. Drain and refresh under cold water.

To prepare the dressing, season the vinegar, then add the oil and dried cherries.

Arrange the asparagus, prosciutto and rocket on individual plates and spoon the dressing over. Serve straightaway.

Chicken roasted with Chilli, Rosemary and Cinnamon

---

2 x 1.3–1.6 kg (3–3½ lb) oven-
   ready free-range chickens
2 sprigs fresh rosemary
2 red chillies
1 x 7.5–10 cm (3–4 inch)
   cinnamon stick, broken up

55 g (2 oz) unsalted butter
sea salt and black pepper
juice of 1 lemon

Preheat the oven to 200°C (fan oven)/220°C (425°F) gas 7. Place the chickens in a roasting tin, and put a sprig of rosemary, a chilli and some cinnamon in the cavity of each bird. Dot the chickens with the butter, season and pour the lemon juice over. Roast for 10 minutes, then turn the oven down to 190°C (fan oven)/200°C (400°F) gas 6 and roast for a further 40–45 minutes, basting occasionally. Leave the chickens to rest out of the oven for 15 minutes before carving.

Tip the juices from inside the chicken into the roasting tin, spooning off some of the fat if it seems excessive. Warm the juices on top of the hob, scraping the bits off the bottom of the tin. Carve the chicken and serve with the juices spooned over.

Garlic Mashed Potato

1 small head of garlic
10 g (¼ oz) unsalted butter
sea salt and black pepper
2 kg (4½ lb) maincrop potatoes

85 ml (3 fl oz) double cream
85 ml (3 fl oz) extra virgin olive
    oil

Put a large pan of salted water on to boil. Cut the top off the head of garlic to reveal the cloves, place it on a small piece of foil, dot with the butter and season. Wrap into an airtight parcel and bake for 30 minutes in the oven with the chicken.

Peel the potatoes, cut into even-size pieces and boil. Drain and press through a sieve or mouli-légumes. Add the cream, olive oil and seasoning.

Squeeze the garlic cloves from their casing and mash into the potato purée. (If preparing the potatoes in advance, add the olive oil after reheating.)

Spring Greens

900 g (2 lb) spring greens
3 tablespoons extra virgin olive
    oil

1 tablespoon lemon juice
sea salt and black pepper

Cut out tough stalks and leaves from greens, and cut the remaining leaves across into strips; wash in a large sink of cold water. Place in a saucepan with a mug of cold water and bring to a simmer, then cover and cook for 5–7 minutes. Drain, pressing out excess water, and dress with the olive oil, lemon juice and seasoning.

Mango Fool with Bitter Chocolate Thins

4 medium-size ripe mangoes,
   about 1.5 kg (3¼ lb) total
1 egg white (size 2)
55 g (2 oz) caster sugar
225 ml (8 fl oz) double cream
2 teaspoons lemon juice

2 teaspoons orange flower
   water (optional)

To serve
dark chocolate thins

Cut off and discard the mango skin; slice the flesh off the stones and purée it in a blender. Pass the purée through a sieve into a large bowl. Whisk the egg white in another bowl; once it has risen whisk in the sugar a tablespoon at a time until you have a stiff, glossy meringue. Whip the cream until it is stiff. Fold the meringue and whipped cream into the mango purée, and gently stir in the lemon juice and orange flower water. Cover and chill until required.

Serve the fool in small bowls surrounded by chocolate thins.

SUMMER DINNER PARTY for 6

Salad of tomatoes with balsamic vinaigrette and anchovies

Salmon and nori lasagne

Souffléed lime pudding with fresh loganberries

A mass of tomatoes arranged together as a salad presents a lavish beauty, and beyond that makes an interesting play on their subtle differences. Choose about four different types: beefsteak, plum, red cherry, yellow pear and so on.

The main course is an update on a personal favourite, lasagne – justly popular, given that it can be prepared in advance, so all you have to do on the day is bung it in the oven in time. The nori affords this particular version a subtle, ocean-sweet fragrance that even the most discerning diner will find hard to pinpoint.

Nori is most familiar to us as the green skin wrapped around sushi. The same seaweed grows on our coasts where it is known as laver, and though the Welsh make a big thing of 'laver bread', a purée of the stuff, it does not seem to have entered our imagination in the same way as the paper-thin Japanese sheets have done.

Nori is available from Japanese and healthfood shops, and more recently I have seen it in supermarkets. Unless labelled *yakinori* (ready toasted), it must first be lightly crisped by passing it over a naked flame or placing it in the oven for a few minutes.

Buy a salmon fillet with the skin on (you can use farmed or wild salmon). For escalopes slice it about 1 cm (1/2 inch) thick as though cutting smoked salmon from a whole side – a task you can always ask your fishmonger to perform.

A word, too, about pudding. No apology has to be made for seasonal cheating: a bowl of assorted berries with some red or white currants draped on top, dusted with icing sugar and served with crème fraîche. Look out for tayberries, loganberries and wild strawberries.

Order of Work
1. Prepare lasagne; put in to bake 20 minutes before sitting down.
2. Make mixture for pudding to stage indicated in recipe.
3. 25 minutes before serving, make first course.
4. As the pudding takes 20 minutes to bake, either finish it before the second course, or straight after.

Salad of Tomatoes with Balsamic Vinaigrette and Anchovies

1.1 kg (2½ lb) assorted
   tomatoes
sea salt and black pepper
caster sugar
9 salted anchovies, halved
   lengthwise
25 g (1 oz) rocket
1 heaped tablespoon snipped
   fresh chives

For the dressing
1 tablespoon balsamic vinegar
6 tablespoons extra virgin olive
   oil

To serve
French bread

Slice the tomatoes, discarding the end slice and the core, or halve if small. Arrange in separate piles on one or two serving platters and sprinkle with salt, pepper and sugar. To prepare the dressing, whisk the vinegar with some seasoning and add the oil.

Tuck the anchovies and rocket leaves between the tomatoes, pour over the dressing and sprinkle with chives. Serve with French bread.

Salmon and Nori Lasagne

350 g (12 oz) lasagne (no pre-cooking variety)

1.1 kg (2½ lb) salmon fillet, sliced into 1 cm (½ inch) escalopes

15 g (½ oz) nori sheets, toasted

85 g (3 oz) Parmesan, freshly grated

For the sauce

200 ml (7 fl oz) white wine

100 g (3½ oz) unsalted butter

85 g (3 oz) plain flour

450 ml (¾ pint) fish stock

450 ml (¾ pint) milk

450 ml (¾ pint) double cream

3 heaped tablespoons freshly grated Parmesan

2 level tablespoons each of finely chopped fresh dill, chervil and parsley

sea salt and black pepper

First prepare the sauce: reduce the wine by half in a medium-size saucepan and reserve. Melt the butter in the same saucepan, add the flour and cook this roux for 1–2 minutes. Remove from the heat and gradually whisk in the fish stock, milk, cream and reduced wine. Bring back to the boil, stirring, and simmer for 5 minutes, stirring occasionally. Add the Parmesan, herbs and seasoning.

Smear some sauce over the bottom of a 25 x 35 x 5 cm (10 x 14 x 2 inch) baking dish, then layer the ingredients as follows: lasagne, sauce, salmon, nori, sauce, lasagne, sauce and so on. In all you should have 3 layers of lasagne, 2 of salmon and 2 of nori, with some sauce either side of each layer of lasagne so that it has enough moisture to cook. Cover with foil. (You can prepare it in advance to this point.)

Preheat the oven to 180°C (fan oven)/190°C (375°F) gas 5. Bake for 30 minutes, then remove the foil, sprinkle the Parmesan over the surface and bake for a further 10 minutes.

Souffléed Lime Pudding with Fresh Loganberries

55 g (2 oz) unsalted butter	85 ml (3 fl oz) milk
85 g (3 oz) plus 2 heaped tablespoons caster sugar	400 g (14 oz) loganberries or raspberries
2 eggs (size 2), separated	icing sugar
25 g (1 oz) plain flour	
finely grated zest and juice of 2 limes	To serve
	whipped cream
85 ml (3 fl oz) double cream	

Cream the butter and 85 g (3 oz) caster sugar together until pale. Incorporate the egg yolks, then the flour, lime zest and juice, cream and milk. Take a large gratin dish, scatter the berries in a single layer over the bottom and sprinkle with the remaining caster sugar. (You can prepare it to this point in advance.)

Preheat the oven to 180°C (fan oven)/190°C (375°F) gas 5 (if you have just baked the lasagne it will already be hot). Stiffly whisk the egg whites and fold them into the soufflé mixture – if you used a food processor to cream the mixture, transfer to a bowl first. Pour the soufflé mixture over the fruit, dust with icing sugar and bake for 20–25 minutes until golden and risen.

Serve straightaway, with whipped cream.

AUTUMN DINNER PARTY for 6

'Little Gem' squashes baked with Gruyère

Pot-roasted monkfish with broad beans 'à la Française'

Blackberry and Champagne compote

Just how did Fanny Craddock cope in those Norman Hartnell ballgowns? Cooking while dressed up goes against the laws of nature. In reality either you or the dinner ends up in a mess. Well, this is a specially designed stay-clean menu where all the last minute action takes place in the oven.

The 'Little Gem' squashes emerge dark and glistening, filled with a rich goo of cheese fondue; some thin, crisp toast to accompany them would not go amiss. The cheese itself can be varied – any of the likes of Beaufort, Appenzeller, Gruyère or Irish Gabriel will do. Or for a milder, but really creamy fondue, use Raclette.

The monkfish is pot-roasted as one large tail section, on the bone, and the result is superbly moist and infused with the scent of bay leaves and garlic. In fact, roasting is something of a misnomer because the fish is cooked with plenty of juices, so it is more steamed than roasted. The vegetables cook alongside the fish, and you end up with a delicious liquor that acts as a sauce. You may want to serve some boiled potatoes tossed with butter to soak it up.

The blackberry and Champagne compote is a dramatic and luxurious deep purple, with just the faintest hint of fizz. I try to keep an emergency packet of *biscuits de Rheims* in my cupboard. These traditional dessert biscuits from Champagne, which are baked in a wood oven, are chunky and roughly hewn, and come in pastel shades. Maison Blanc pâtisseries usually have a good selection.

Order of Work

1. Prepare the blackberry and Champagne compote to the point indicated.
2. Prepare the squashes and the pot-roasted monkfish to the point indicated in each recipe.
3. 30 minutes before sitting down, place the squashes in the oven; after 20 minutes put in the monkfish to roast. If serving potatoes put these on to boil.
4. Finish the dessert immediately before eating it.

'Little Gem' Squashes baked with Gruyère

---

280 g (10 oz) Gruyère, grated
85 ml (3 fl oz) double cream
2 teaspoons Kirsch

sea salt and black pepper
6 'Little Gem' squashes, each
   the size of a grapefruit

Blend the Gruyère, cream, Kirsch and seasoning in a bowl. Slice the tops off the squashes and scoop out the seeds from each one using your fingers. Fill to within 5 mm (1/4 inch) of the top with the cheese mixture, packing it down firmly. Remove the seeds from the tops of the squash and put the tops back in place. Place the squash on a baking tray. Prepare to this point in advance.

Preheat the oven to 200°C (fan oven)/220°C (425°F) gas 7 and bake for 30 minutes. Serve each person one squash.

Pot-roasted Monkfish with Broad Beans 'à la Française'

---

1 x 1.3 kg (3 lb) monkfish tail	4 leeks
2 cloves garlic, peeled and sliced	55 g (2 oz) unsalted butter
6 bay leaves	85 ml (3 fl oz) white wine
sea salt and black pepper	85 ml (3 fl oz) fish or vegetable stock
450 g (1 lb) frozen young broad beans	chopped fresh flat-leaf parsley to garnish
3 'Little Gem' lettuces	

Slice the membrane and any coloured flesh off the monkfish tail as neatly as possible, leaving the white fish on the bone. Make 6 diagonal slits either side of the central bone, on one side of the fish only. Place a garlic sliver in alternate slits, and a bay leaf in the others. Season all over with salt and pepper and set aside.

Bring a pan of water to the boil and cook the broad beans; drain and reserve. Trim the base of the lettuces, discard the outside leaves and cut each lettuce lengthways into 6 wedges. Trim the leeks to retain the white and pale green parts and remove the tough outer layers, then cut into fine strips 5–7.5 cm (2–3 inches) long.

Preheat the oven to 200°C (fan oven)/220°C (425°F) gas 7. Melt the butter in a large heavy casserole (eg Le Creuset) and sweat the lettuce and leeks for 5 minutes, seasoning them and stirring frequently. Put the monkfish in with the vegetables, pour over the wine and stock and cover with the lid. Prepare to this point in advance.

Transfer to the oven and cook for 30 minutes. Ten minutes before the end of cooking, remove the casserole lid and stir the broad beans in with the braised vegetables. Season again.

To serve, divide the fish up and serve it with the vegetables, surrounded by boiled potatoes, if serving, and sprinkled with parsley.

Blackberry and Champagne Compote

900 g (2 lb) blackberries
85 g (3 oz) caster sugar
200 ml (7 fl oz) demi-sec
   Champagne

To serve
crème fraîche
dessert biscuits

Place 400 g (14 oz) of blackberries in a blender or food processor with the sugar and reduce to a purée. Pass through a sieve into a bowl. Mix the remaining whole blackberries into the purée. Prepare to this point in advance.

To serve, stir the Champagne into the compote and spoon it into glass bowls. Place a dollop of crème fraîche on top of each and accompany with dessert biscuits.

WINTER DINNER PARTY for 6

Eggs en cocotte with creamed chicory

Halibut with fines herbes and orange in olive oil, and saffron potatoes

Fresh goat's cheese and honey with date madeleines

Does anyone ever grow out of eggs *en cocotte*, cooked to perfection: that age-old treat of dipping toast into a warm and runny yolk, just set on the outside. Here it comes with the additional surprise of a bed of chicory braised with cream, flavoured with freshly chopped dill and chives.

The halibut that follows merits the simplest treatment – accentuate its succulence by smothering it with olive oil. The key is that the oil must be good, though both gentle and strong oils can work. Also, warm it to marginally above blood temperature; any more and all will be lost. Add a little sparkle with just a small amount of orange, plus some *fines herbes*.

For the pudding I use a Cabri goat's cheese, which is not too salty, and cover it with a resinous lime-tree honey. Eaten with date madeleines warm from the oven, this tastes fabulously exotic in the midst of a cold winter.

Order of Work

1. Prepare and chill the date madeleine mixture. Ideally, the madeleines should be baked between the main course and dessert, but if you prefer, bake them in advance.
2. Prepare the creamed chicory.
3. Prepare the ingredients for the sauce, and the fish ready for steaming; peel the potatoes.
4. 20 minutes before you want to eat, bake the eggs en cocotte. Put the potatoes on to boil when you sit down.
5. Warm the sauce and steam the fish while clearing away the first course.

Eggs en Cocotte with Creamed Chicory

550 g (1¼ lb) Belgian chicory	sea salt and black pepper
1 tablespoon extra virgin olive oil	1 heaped tablespoon finely chopped fresh dill
1 large clove garlic, peeled and sliced	1 heaped tablespoon finely chopped fresh chives
2 teaspoons lemon juice	1 level tablespoon freshly grated Parmesan
150 ml (¼ pint) plus 2 table-spoons double cream	6 eggs (size 2)

Finely slice the chicory crossways until you reach the hard inner centre two-thirds of the way down; halve this lengthways and then slice. Work quickly to avoid its discolouring. Heat the olive oil in a frying pan over a high heat, add the garlic and, moments later, the chicory and sauté for 3 minutes. Turn the heat down to moderate. Add the lemon juice, 150 ml (¼ pint) cream and seasoning, cover and cook for 5 minutes. Then remove the lid and cook for about 10 minutes until the sauce is thick. Stir in the herbs and Parmesan. You can prepare this in advance and reheat before the next stage.

Preheat the oven to 180°C (fan oven)/190°C (375°F) gas 5. Divide the hot chicory mixture among 6 individual ramekins or bowls, making a well, and break an egg into each one. Spoon the remaining 2 tablespoons of cream over the egg and season. Place in a bain-marie, filling with boiling water to come three-quarters of the way up the sides of the ramekins, and cook in the oven for 8–10 minutes until the egg white is just set; the yolk should remain runny. Serve with toast and butter.

Halibut with Fines Herbes and Orange in Olive Oil, and Saffron Potatoes

6 x 175–225 g (6–8 oz) halibut
  fillets, skinned
sea salt and black pepper

For the sauce
2 small oranges
150 ml (¼ pint) extra virgin
  olive oil
1 tablespoon lemon juice or
  Seville orange juice

For the fines herbes
1 level teaspoon finely
  chopped fresh tarragon
2 teaspoons finely chopped
  fresh chervil
1 tablespoon finely chopped
  fresh chives
1 tablespoon finely chopped
  fresh flat-leaf parsley

For the potatoes
¼ teaspoon ground saffron
1.3 kg (3 lb) salad or new
  potatoes, peeled

Cut the skin and pith off the oranges; remove segments with a knife, cut into small pieces and reserve. Mix together the fines herbes.

Bring a pan of salted water to the boil, add the saffron and boil the potatoes until cooked; drain.

Season the halibut and steam for 4–5 minutes.

To finish the sauce, gently heat the olive oil until warm; add the orange, lemon juice, fines herbes and seasoning and allow 1 minute to warm through before serving. Serve the fish with the sauce spooned over, accompanied by the potatoes.

Fresh Goat's Cheese and Honey with Date Madeleines

225 g (8 oz) fresh goat's
  cheese
jar of lime-tree honey, or any
  other strong-flavoured
  variety

For the madeleines (makes
  12–14)
2 eggs (size 2)
70 g (2½ oz) caster sugar
25 g (1 oz) vanilla sugar
finely grated zest of 1 lemon

55 g (2 oz) plain flour
pinch of salt
1 level teaspoon baking
  powder
55 g (2 oz) ground almonds
115 g (4 oz) unsalted butter,
  melted, plus extra for
  greasing
175 g (6 oz) dates, stoned and
  chopped
icing sugar for dusting

Whisk the eggs and both sugars together until pale. Add the lemon zest. Sift together the flour, salt and baking powder, and fold these and the ground almonds into the egg mixture; do not overwork. Gently mix in the melted butter and dates. Leave the mixture to rest in a cool place for at least 30 minutes.

Preheat the oven to 190°C (fan oven)/200°C (400°F) gas 6. Brush fairy cake moulds – or scallop-shaped madeleine moulds if you have them – with melted butter, and spoon in the mixture so the moulds are two-thirds full. Bake for 10 minutes until golden and risen. Loosen with a knife and turn on to a rack to cool. Dust with icing sugar and serve warm.

Serve the goat's cheese with the honey spooned over (if your honey has set, stand the jar in hot water until it becomes runny). Accompany with the date madeleines.

COCKTAIL PARTIES

I am going to restrict this section to a few words of advice. This is perhaps the most daunting type of entertaining at home: it is not coincidental that if the party is big enough and you're feeling flush enough you are going to call in the professionals.

As a broad guideline, try to have a mix of hot and cold appetisers, and there are more don'ts than dos: avoid stuffed mangetouts and cherry tomatoes, avoid roulades, avoid filling choux puffs, avoid tempura, tail-on prawns and quails' eggs, and don't do anything too witty.

The point is that cocktail appetisers can run to seriously intricate little creations, especially canapés, and the chances are that if someone is engrossed in conversation they won't be taking that much notice of what they are eating or how much time has been invested in threading, spreading, decorating and crowning. But enough of such cynicism.

CROSTINI

Crostini have more or less replaced old-fashioned canapés and are far easier to contemplate. You can make them any size that suits – tiny, and hand them around on a tray, or finger-buffet size (dreadful expression) if you are trying to bridge the gap between cocktail snacks and dinner.

To begin with you need a crisp, golden bread base. For small crostini I usually cut them from a thinly sliced loaf of white bread using a biscuit cutter. For larger ones I thinly slice French sticks of various diameters.

Lay these on a baking sheet and dry them out in the oven for 5 minutes at 180°C (fan oven)/190°C (375°F) gas 5, then paint them with olive oil or clarified butter and bake for a further 10–12 minutes until they are pale gold in colour.

The spread should be conspicuous in flavour, really pungent. There is no excuse for not running up a bowl of tapenade, the salty, black olive purée from the Med: 115 g (4 oz) stoned black olives – try to use the wrinkled Provençal variety that slip off the stone with ease, 15 g (½ oz) capers, a pinch of thyme, ½ clove garlic, and a little olive oil and black pepper; reduce this to a paste in a food processor. Sometimes I add a spoonful of crème fraîche to lighten it.

Pesto, too, must be home-made; the shop-bought stuff is pretty filthy. Other spreads that spring to mind are hummus, a smoky aubergine dip like baba ghanoush, taramasalata, and a broad bean purée spiced with toasted and ground cumin. Really quick answers are feta mashed with a little olive oil, lemon juice and chilli, or Stilton mashed with olive oil and decorated with walnuts.

You will need some sort of frivolity in the way of a garnish, but this need not be more than a few strips of roasted red peppers, halved olives, capers, some chopped fresh herbs or a dusting of cayenne pepper.

The most basic crostini I can name transports me to the olive mills of southern Sicily. There, during the olive harvest, should you visit an oil press you will be greeted by a flurry of activity as an upturned crate is set up by way of a table, and on it are placed some freshly baked bread, a jar of sea salt and dried oregano, and a jug of the newly pressed olive oil, which at this point is powerfully green and peppery.

First you toast the bread, sometimes over an open fire, then liberally douse it in olive oil and spinkle over salt and oregano. You can replicate this as an appetiser with small pieces of toast, or pitta bread. Fine shavings of bottarga or strips of anchovy could replace the herbs.

The other 'on toast' appetiser that never fails is Welsh rarebit.

DEEP-FRIED MORSELS

Hell for the home-kitchen. For this one you need a dedicated chef who is going to stand attendant by the stove, dipping, frying, draining and salting, and then rushing the morsels out to the party. Apart from the fact that you will end up smelling like a chip-shop, if you neglect the hot fat you may end up with fire. So, unless you have called in additional help forget this side of things.

The good news is that supermarkets do a good job of pre-packed Chinese and Indian items that can be reheated in the oven. The quality of some of these is surprisingly good, and being such a specialised field you are probably better off buying them in any case. Marks and Spencer excel at this type of food; Waitrose are pretty good too. Amoy is a brand that knows what it is doing.

All you need is a small bowl of Kikkoman soy sauce in which to dip the morsels, or you could serve the sweet and sour Thai dipping sauce on page 42.

TARTS AND PIZZA

In my catering days I regularly used to find myself assembling miniature quiches, little tarts filled with a few diced vegetables in a sabayon, or mince pies at Christmastime. I cannot imagine doing any such thing for my own parties. But quiches and pizza do make superb appetisers, the answer here being to make large ones and cut them up into pieces.

The main point when making quiches is to prebake the pastry shell until it is almost cooked. Once it is filled with custard it cannot brown any further, so be sure that it is lightly tanned and crisp before you fill it.

I rarely consult recipes for the egg custard filling – just blend to taste a mix of double cream, milk and any cooking juices or stock that are relevant. Add egg yolks and a minimal amount of whole egg (this is the enemy of a quiche, setting the custard rock hard, while egg yolks retain a very loose, unctuous set). Filling ingredients can range from diced lobster, crab meat, mussels or oysters to diced tomato, broad beans, pieces of asparagus, feta or Gruyère cheese – all of which should be accompanied by a good addition of chopped fresh herbs to the custard.

When it comes to pizzas, obviously you can use a bread dough base, but I also resort to puff pastry, weighting it with foil and baking beans and cooking it until it is crisp. For a pissaladière, I make a reduced fresh tomato purée, spread it on the base and decorate with stoned and quartered black olives and fresh marjoram leaves.

OUT OF A PACKET

There is a lot to be said for 70s-style dips and crisps. I rely on a basic recipe handed down to me by my mother: a 200 g (7 oz) packet of Philadelphia cream cheese, 1 tablespoon lemon juice, 2 tablespoons single cream and also of milk, 1 teaspoon chopped onion and a dash of Tabasco; reduce to a smooth purée in a food processor, then cover and chill. Whisk before serving – it should be the consistency of whipped cream – and dust with cayenne pepper.

You could serve crudités with this. Never buy these, because they will be dried out and woody where they have been cut. You end up having to trim them, and at this point you might as well make them freshly. Do not worry too much about arranging five or six different vegetables; one or two in quantity will look more arresting – say radishes and carrots.

Healthfood shops are the best hunting ground for crisps, where they tend to be freer from additives. I have a particular fondness for corn chips, blue, yellow and red, and for little rice cakes flavoured with sea salt and sesame seeds. In fact, these can double up as the base for canapés.

Always have some nuts and olives: salted almonds, cashews, pistachios and macadamias. You can arrange different types of olive on a platter, maybe with some pickled chillies and cubes of feta, separating the piles with sprigs of herbs.

LUXURY

The key word for cocktail parties is luxury: lots of smoked salmon, air-dried ham, good salamis, oysters and scallops, plus caviar for a real treat (sevruga is the strongest in flavour; save the beluga for another time). Salmon keta roe is wonderful too.

INDEX

Raclette cheese 168
Radishes and butter 116
Rappie pie with sorrel sauce 62–3
Raspberry(ies)
  compote with pear and Greek
    yoghurt 19
  melon filled with passionfruit and
    20
  Roger Vergé's raspberry dressing
    103
  with tira-mi-su and praline 78–9
Rhubarb compote and cinnamon
  toast 23
Rick Stein's mouclade 134
Rice
  mussel risotto with basil cream
    138–9
  and peas 74
  wild rice salad with baby corn,
    coriander and almonds 72
  wild rice salad with langoustines
    107
Ricotta cheese with fresh figs, honey
  and almonds 17
Risotto, mussel, with basil cream
  138–9
Rocket
  asparagus and prosciutto 159, 160
  with barbequed figs and Parma
    ham 102
  potato salad with char-grilled tuna
    and 107, 113
  salad of smoked eel, capers and 69
Roger Vergé's raspberry dressing with
  green salad 103

Sabayon 181
  champagne, with oysters and
    herbed noodles 141
Saffron and honey custard 152
Saffron potatoes 73, 172, 174
Sake 108, 110
Salad dressing
  balsamic 140
  Roger Vergé's raspberry 103
  sesame seed 147
Salads
  asparagus and peas, with tomato
    and basil 112
  Caesar 84, 89
  chicken and French beans 147

  cucumber 66
  green, with Roger Vergé's raspberry
    dressing 103
  mixed leaves with deep-fried herbs
    71
  Pan molle with anchovies 90
  porcini 127
  potato 107, 113
  Puy lentils 149
  smoked eel, capers and rocket 69
  smoky aubergine, with cinnamon
    goat's cheese 91
  Tabbouleh, with green mango 104
  tomato 106
  tomato with anchovies 164, 165
  wild rice, with baby corn,
    coriander and almonds 72
  wild rice, with langoustines 107
  winter chicories, fennel and blood
    oranges 70
Salads, warm,
  new potatoes, oysters and chervil
    123
  poached salmon, baby spinach and
    asparagus 140
Salami 116, 183
  with salad of Puy lentils 149
Salmon 84
  carpaccio of salmon with dill 122
  fishcakes and lemon butter sauce
    40–1
  keta roe 183
  and nori lasagne 164, 166
  teriyaki 110
  warm salad of baby spinach,
    asparagus and poached 140
  see also Smoked salmon
Salsa
  pineapple and date, with duck
    146
  red pepper, with squid 94
  tomato, with avocado soup 84, 86
Samphire 84
  blanched 48
Sardines 85, 106
  spice-fried 41
Sauces
  chocolate-clove 157–8
  lemon butter 40–1
  roasted tomato 50
  sorrel 62–3

MORE TASTE THAN TIME